THE
COURAGE
TO LIVE
YOUR
DREAMS

THE
COURAGE
TO LIVE
YOUR
DREAMS

LES BROWN

MEDIA

Published 2021 by Gildan Media LLC
aka G&D Media
www.GandDmedia.com

First Edition: 2021

Front Cover design by Tom McKeveny

Interior design by Meghan Day Healey of Story Horse, LLC.

Library of Congress Cataloging-in-Publication Data is available upon request

ISBN: 978-1-7225-0507-3

10   9   8   7   6   5   4   3   2   1

Contents

one
REINVENT YOUR LIFE..................................7

two
SAY YES TO YOUR DREAMS..................23

three
POWERFUL GOALS..................................37

four
A COMMITMENT TO HAPPINESS.........53

five
THE RIGHT PEOPLE................................67

six
WHATEVER IT TAKES 81

seven

BECOME A POWERFUL PERSON........95

eight

FIND A CAUSE 111

nine

THE COURAGE TO
CONFRONT YOUR FEARS.................. 123

ten

GETTING UNSTUCK–
OVERCOMING PROBLEMS................. 139

eleven

YOU GOTTA BE HUNGRY...................... 151

twelve

PUT IT ALL TOGETHER 167

o n e

REINVENT YOUR LIFE

I know that you've got greatness within you. I know that you have unlimited potential. I know that you have something to give to the universe. You are more than capable of making this your decade.

It's time for you to look within yourself and decide "I'm in charge of my destiny. I'm in charge here and I'm not going to allow anybody to turn me around. I am determined that I'm going to make it."

This is the only life you've got, so you don't want to squander it doing something you don't want to do just because you feel you can't do any better. You *can* do better. You *should* do better. You *deserve* to do better. You are entitled to that. That is your right to do better.

One of the things you will discover is that many people go through life unthinkingly, just drifting from day to day, not really being aware of who they are and what the possibilities are for their lives. Take a moment right now and think about yourself. Just think about things you have done that you have never given any thought to because you've been doing them for so long. I'll give you an example. When I lived in Columbus Ohio I used to drive twelve miles to work every day from my house. There were many mornings that I would get out of my car, go inside, put the key in the door and then ask myself this question, how did I get here? Though I had driven there I was not consciously aware of how I got there. I'd done it for so long; I didn't even have to think about it.

Now think about your life for a moment. How many things have you been doing unconsciously? Maybe you've had a similar experience to mine. When I realized this unconsciousness in my behavior, I started looking at myself and at different areas of my life. Many of us do things that we just don't think about. We believe that's just the way we are and we can become locked into a particular habit or behavior. Human beings have the capacity for great change. If it's something negative it can be changed. If it's positive, we can improve on it, we can build on it.

Think about yourself right now. Is your life what you want it to be? If it is not, you have the consciousness, you have the power within you to reinvent your life, and you should. If you are the same person today that you were yesterday or the day before or a year ago, then you're not growing. Your life is going up or it's going down. You're either saying hello or you're saying goodbye. Take a look at you right now. What is it that you could be doing if you decided to free yourself up, if you decided to confront your fears, if you decided to become consciously aware of what you're doing right now?

I used to have a tremendous temper. It did not take much to set me off. I decided to become consciously aware of what was happening to me physically. I felt my heart beating faster, my breath getting shorter, and I decided, "Wait. Cool out. Take a walk." I used to fence, and fencing is a gentleman's sport. My coach used to say, "If you find yourself losing your temper, stop, make a tap on the floor with your foil and leave the court." We have to learn to activate the thinker in ourselves— to catch ourselves going on automatic. This is crucial if we want to change, to get into a different groove, and to find a different path for our lives.

Look at yourself right now. What are you doing on a day to day basis? Is it producing the kind of results that you want in your life? Look closely at one area of your life. It might be in your relationship, in your work life, or your personal organization. Maybe you're surrounded by all types of clutter and you want to become neater in your appearance or how you're handling your environment. Whatever it is, identify just one area of your life that you want to focus your time and energy to improve right now.

Let's look at improving your attitude as our first example. I have found it is very important to develop conscious awareness of our thoughts. We cannot control the thoughts that come into our minds, but we can control the thoughts that we dwell on. Without conscious awareness of our thoughts we will constantly find ourselves in a negative state of mind. If you look at the news, if you listen to conversations, and just look at the world in general, you realize how often we are surrounded with all kinds of negativity. If your goal is to develop a more positive attitude, you must work consciously to improve your outlook, regardless of what's going on around you. How can we exist in the world and not allow the world to exist in us? This is going to be very challenging because things will happen that will test you. You will become aware of things you weren't aware of before.

Pay attention to your attitude right now. What are things that you allow to trigger your attitude? John

Powell has a powerful illustration of this in his book, *Why Am I Afraid to Tell You Who I Am?* A fellow went to buy a newspaper, and the clerk was very rude to him yet he remained courteous to the clerk. His companion asked, "Why were you so polite and courteous to that clerk considering how rude he was to you?" He replied, "I am not going to allow that man or anybody to determine how I'm going to act."

That is the power that we have. You can decide from this day forward not to allow circumstances, events, people, or any type of news to determine how you're going to react. You are in charge. Decide to become consciously aware of everything that's happening in your life right now. Become an observer of life and yourself and you will realize that you can look, you can observe, and you can choose to respond positively. Realize that you are in charge.

Remember that to consciously change requires daily work. It's not going to be easy. There will be off days. Learn to monitor your thinking, which helps develop awareness of our habits—the things that we find ourselves doing without thinking. Habits are crafty, they sneak up on us. That's why you've got to catch yourself and monitor yourself constantly. Observe yourself and begin to say, "Hey, how am I doing?" Do it in the moment. Don't try and project too far ahead. Just try and stay on top of yourself on a day-to-day basis in the various moments you find yourself in.

Look at the things you want to do and decide that you're going to become the active force in your life. Decide that you will not go through life feeling like a victim. Decide that when things become challenging that you're not going to personalize it, you're going to look at it and work things out and learn from it. Learn from it. That's the key. If you've lost your job, don't say, "I've been laid off," rather, "I've been given an opportunity by the universe to find my life work."

As you view all of the things that happen to you as an opportunity, you're now taking it from a different perspective. Now you are becoming an active force in your life. Rather than running from things as they begin to change, you become a change driver. You know that you've got the power within you to make the difference. This force, this power, this energy that you have, is more powerful than anything that can ever happen to you. You're more powerful than your circumstances or anything that you experience right now. Decide that you're going to commit yourself to act on your ideas, to become happy. Commit yourself to live your dream. Commit yourself to become the architect of your future.

Here's something that Goethe wrote that I love very much, "Until one is committed, there is hesitancy, the chance to draw back, always ineffectiveness." You must be willing to jump out there. Don't ask, "How do I do that?" First you make the commitment. Once you make a commitment, then life will give you some answers. You can't sit on the side of the pool and just stick your toe in. You have to be willing to make the leap. Most people don't want to do that. They want to sit on the side and say, "Is it cold out there? Is it rough out there?" To which I say, "Come on out and see."

Decide to make that commitment. That's when you begin. You become involved in the learning process. In *The Second Himalayan Expedition*, famed Scottish mountaineer W.H. Murray said, "Concerning all acts of initiative and creation there is one elementary truth, the ignorance of which kills countless ideas and splendid plans: that the moment one definitely commits oneself, then providence moves too. All sorts of things occur to help one that would not otherwise have occurred. A whole stream of events issues from the decision raising in one's favor all manner of unforeseen incidents and meetings and material assistance which no man would have dreamed would come his way. I have learned a deep respect for one of Goethe's couplets: 'Whatever you can do or dream you can, begin it. Boldness has genius, magic, and power in it.'" Begin it now.

Minister and influential thought leader Dr. Johnnie Colemon said, "It works if you work it." As you start looking at your life and working on your dream, you're going to nurture that idea. There will be people who criticize you, who don't see it for you. Don't let them turn you around. That's key because people *will* try to turn you around. Like the traditional blues song says, "Ain't gonna let nobody turn me around." This is one of the reasons people don't act on their dreams and ideas.

When I'm talking with kids that are in institutions and ask, "What happened? Why did you give up working hard and making good grades?" Some will answer, "Well, they started teasing me." The kids allowed peer pressure to cause them to scale down their dreams and their ambitions. They started following the crowd. That's why many people don't do the things they want to do. A friend of mine wanted to become an actor all his life. He let someone convince him that he couldn't become an actor. They told him that Hollywood would swallow him up. That it's too competitive, that there are thousands of unemployed people out there.

Another friend decided at age forty-two that she was going to "live her dream." Her son had graduated from high school, and she decided to take the plunge and go to Hollywood. She's a very quiet person and had no experience in acting. She decided to make the commitment and is now working on a one-woman show, getting support from everywhere because she was willing to make the commitment. The other guy

I mentioned is far more talented and skillful, but he wasn't willing to make the commitment. So now he goes to work every day at a job that's making him sick, all because he doesn't have the guts or the boldness to stand up in life and say, "I am going to live my dream."

All of us have experiences of being stuck—things that happen to us and we become like a broken record. A particular instance or event continues to reoccur and holds us at a different point in our lives mentally, emotionally, spiritually or financially. Let me recount a woeful tale as an illustration of being stuck.

There was a well-known figure in Ohio, a fellow who was known as "chicken man." Chicken man used to drive around in a station wagon, with flashing lights and a chicken toy on top. Dressed in feathers and a strange hat, he rode around with a baby carriage and two baby dolls. He would get out of the car, make chicken sounds and then continue on his way. None of us knew anything about him and he was the object of much teasing and ridicule. One day, I met someone who knew him and learned his story. While asleep one night, he smelled smoke and awoke to his house engulfed in flames. Panicked, he ran outside, and then heard the screaming of his two daughters still in the house. He tried to go back for them, despite the raging flames, going for the doors, the windows, any way he could. People had to restrain him; it was the most desperate and terrifying scene.

Shortly after, an uncle of the girls arrived and asked where they were. When learning their fate he began to beat their father, yelling, "You fool, you coward, you chicken, you chicken, you chicken." The uncle beat him to the ground and he never fought back. When they helped him up he did not speak at first. Then he began to make the sound of a chicken and never stopped. He took those little baby dolls and carriage around downtown Columbus every day and made the sounds of a chicken. This is a horrendous tragedy and we can understand why this man became stuck.

I believe in the human spirit and that it has the capacity to overcome overwhelming catastrophe. Go through the grieving, go through the anger and the heartbreak. Experience what you must experience. Learn what you must learn. Then learn to live. Learn to get on with your life.

I believe that we all have greatness within us that we were endowed with and the only way we can discover it is to constantly challenge ourselves. Many people never discover their greatness because they become satisfied. They stop growing. They stop learning. They stop developing themselves. They stop stretching. In order to discover your true greatness, don't allow life to lull you to sleep.

Constantly look at yourself and ask, "How can life use me more effectively? How is it that I can begin to stretch out? What talents or skills am I not using right now?" I was talking with a friend the other day and I asked her, "If the unthinkable were to happen to you what is it that you want to do?" She asked, "What do you mean?" I said, "What if you came to work one day and the corporation was closed? Due to a merger or restructuring or downsizing or because of financial problems, they're out of business?" She said, "I don't know. I guess I'll go look for another job." I said, "Wait a minute now. Let's look at this."

Here's what she was doing. She was looking at herself as an employee, as opposed to looking at herself as a company, You Incorporated. I'm suggesting that you do that. Look at yourself as You Incorporated. Look at the place where you work as your client. This is your customer, and they pay you for providing a service for them. I don't care if it's clerical or administrative; whatever role that you're working in—as a marketing representative or salesperson—you provide a service that affects their bottom line. Now, look at yourself and ask yourself the question "What other customers could I begin to create and develop for myself in the event the unthinkable happens, like this particular business going under? What is it that you can do?

Ask yourself what skills you have. Do you have leadership skills? Are you the person who is able to organize the bowling league? What about your communication skills or your ability to get along with people? You may have good people skills in other areas of your life that you're not using right now. I have a friend who's a very meticulous person, very organized. Whenever we decide we want something organized, we call him and say, "Hey, we want you to handle this," because he has a proclivity for detail and for staying on top of things. However, he has never used his talents and abilities for himself. He does it for a neighborhood group or a club or organization, but never for himself. Yet he could. He could earn money as a consultant, teaching other people how to become more organized, how to be an effective planner, how to manage tasks.

What talents or abilities do you have that you're not doing anything with? I'm reminded of the story about a great artist. This man played piano very well, and had a good following, playing in nightclubs. One night a patron demanded he sing a song but he said, "I'll play anything you want, but I don't sing," and continued playing. The crowd insisted that they were tired of hearing him play and wanted to have some singing. Finally the bartender said, "If you want to get paid, sing something. My patrons want to hear some singing." So the piano player began to sing. And no one has ever sung the song *Sweet Lorraine* better than Nat King Cole.

What talent are you sitting on? Ask yourself, can you do more than you're doing now? If you're really honest, you'll say yes. If you allowed yourself to remove the fears, the doubts, and the negative inner conversation, what are the other things you could be doing? If you freed yourself up and gave yourself permission what things could you do? In my particular case, I was sitting in the audience watching the great motivational speaker Zig Ziglar going back and forth on stage, talking to over 2,000 people. I said to myself, "I could do that. I've always enjoyed talking to people." What is it that you could be doing right now? I want you to hold a vision of that?

I want you to tenaciously hold that vision because that vision of yourself, of doing and living and experiencing what you have right now is very important. Most people don't have a vision beyond where they are right now. They can't see themselves doing more and achieving more. I want you to have this larger vision of yourself. This is different than having a positive mental attitude. Many people have been conditioned to have a narrow vision of themselves and are convinced that what they're doing right now is all they are capable of doing. I want you to project yourself into the future. And before you ask yourself the next key question I want you to think about this important statement: you don't get in life what you want; you get in life what you are.

The key question is: What kind of person must you become? What has to change about you? What is it that you must do? What type of preparation is important? What is it that you need to do right now that will help you develop the level of consciousness to produce those results or to become that kind of person? Here's something else I want you to do. Look at the vision you have of yourself or the area you want to venture into. How can you earn money doing it even if it's a habit or something that you simply love to do?

I have a friend who loved to cook and bake. Burma Stewart baked a mean cheese cake. Christmastime or Thanksgiving, whenever people wanted a cheese cake they would call her. Burma was a single parent, working on a job and not at all happy with what she was doing. I said, "Burma, why don't you start charging for those cheesecakes?" So she did just that. She started a business and provided gourmet cheesecakes to restaurants all over northeast Ohio. She became wildly successful, based on something she just loved to do.

Identify something that is achievable, something you know that you can do, and do that. When you do, it builds up your confidence to do something else that's a little bit more challenging—something that will make you stretch a bit more. Then do that. As you continue to mushroom and take on more challenges, you will conjure up the best in you. As you continue to do this and get into the flow of things, you begin to expand and develop your consciousness through those experiences. Don't be afraid to fail. Don't be afraid to make mistakes. I think that most people allow their fear of failure or making mistakes or looking awkward to discourage them from trying to do anything. You're not going to be perfect. You're going to make a lot of mistakes, but let that be an education for you. Let that be something that you can look at and say, "Hey, I learned something from that."

Look at your life, and decide to become an active force in it. Decide to embrace whatever is required on your part, whatever development, preparation, or challenges you must take on. You're going to face the disapproval of friends, the rejection, the ridicule, the laughter, the sarcastic remarks, the cynicism. Decide that it doesn't matter to you. When you find that there's something you want to do and people start saying "You can't do it," remember successful businessman Dexter Yager who said, "When the dream is big enough, the odds don't matter." Go for your dream.

You're going to have long periods of not being able to see the light at the end of the tunnel. There will be times you're going to get bruised and knocked down. I have this old saying that when life knocks you down, try to land on your back, because if you can look up, you can get up. I love what George Burns said, "I'd rather fail at doing something I love than succeed at doing something I hate."

There's a feeling that you get within when you resolve, "I'm going to conquer this mountain and if I don't, I'll die on the side trying."

As you continue to pursue your goal there will be a time that you begin to realize your goal has almost become secondary. What you become in the process of pursuing your goal has far more meaning and value than the goal itself. You can go to sleep at night with a clear conscience that you gave it your all, that you live life on your terms. You can smile as you say "I gave it the best that I have."

two

SAY YES TO YOUR DREAMS

As you begin to look toward the future and look at yourself right now, it's very important to say yes to whatever dreams you have of doing more and experiencing more, because when you do that, you are literally extending your life. You're adding more quality and richness and fullness to your life. I want you to practice constantly looking at where you could be, if you gave yourself permission. Many people, once they reach a certain level, stop and relax and lay back on their laurels. Look at your life right now and look into the future and constantly hold a larger vision where you are doing more and achieving more. Just look at yourself and start using your imagination to see the universe as your playground where you're going to come out and challenge yourself to do more and use all your talents and skills.

I want you to realize that when you say you want to do something that's beyond your comfort zone, that will trigger some inner conversations—and 87% of those inner conversations are negative conversations. There was a study conducted with a swim team at UCLA where they told a group their scores were not good. They then observed that those swimmers whose scores improved reported thinking, "Hey, it was a fluke, I can do better than that," and they did just that. Others were susceptible to negative thoughts, "Hey, I'm not as good as I thought I was," and their scores showed just that. How many times have you talked yourself out of doing something? It took nine years for me to act on that first thought I could become a public speaker. After that first conversation within myself when I said that I can do this, I then allowed the negative part of me, that lower consciousness to dominate my thinking and that's what I responded to.

When you have negative conversations that are building a logical case as to why you *cannot* live your dream—you don't have the money or the training or the contacts, you don't have what it takes and you're not good enough—you must learn to ignore those conversations. Then start building a positive case on why you can do it, and start looking at what the things are that you need to work on.

Many times you can have a "Yes, I can" attitude, but a "No, I can't" aptitude. Make sure that you don't hype yourself up and go forward trying to pursue your dream without proper preparation. Once you determine what it is you want to do and you hold the vision, and you've looked at what you need to do to develop yourself, write down your goals. A lot of people just never take the time to do that.

This is what I do—I write down my goals and I read them three times a day. Why would I do that? I believe that whatever you hold in consciousness, whatever you focus on, that is what you're going to begin to multiply and produce in your life experience. Denis Waitley, author of *The Psychology of Winning*, would say that what we have in our lives is a result of our current dominant thinking. In order to change the results we have I like to repeat the saying of Jack Boland, creator of *The Master Mind Principle*, "If you want to keep on getting what you're getting, keep on doing what you're doing." We want to feed our mind some different types of thoughts and different types of visions. Write your goals down and read them three times a day. Embrace the vision you have for yourself. Hold it constantly, tenaciously, even when you have no evidence to support it. Feed yourself with motivational books and tapes, and talk to yourself to drown out those inner conversations that are negative. Start saying yes to yourself by drowning out those conversations. Talk to yourself, and don't talk casually. Speak with power, feeling, and conviction because you want to begin to override and short circuit that lower part and begin to express the higher self, that higher consciousness to tap that unlimited power, that boundless energy that you showed up with, that you were endowed with.

You came with everything you need. Buckminster Fuller said "Every child is born a genius, but the process of living de-geniuses them." Because of the damage we receive from life where we're told more about our limitations than our potential, most of us go to our graves and take our music with us. As you affirm your right to express more and to experience more in life, let the words of Robert Browning about releasing the "imprisoned splendor," guide you to your future with this larger vision—to saying yes to your dreams. Write down your dreams. Write them in detail and be exact in what you want. There's a story of a football team that had a goal of going to the Super Bowl. Then they went and they got whipped. They should have said, "Our goal is to go to the Super Bowl and win." Be exact.

I believe that all of us came here with something. All of us showed up to give something and nobody but you is going to give that service that you have to give.

No one's going to produce your product. No one's going to write your book. No one's going to open your academy. No one's going to create your daycare with a special curriculum to cultivate the high self-esteem in our children. That's your idea. If you don't bring your idea out here before you die, all of us will suffer because we've been deprived of your genius. You will take it to your grave with you. That's what most people do.

There is a quote attributed to Benjamin Franklin, "Some people die at 25 and aren't buried until 75." They're walking dead. You can tell by the way they walk, how they look in the face, when they speak to you. People who make it in life have energy. You've got to have life. If you're excited about what you're doing, you will convince yourself and others.

Let's look at the area of sales. People don't buy because of logical reasoning. People buy because of the way they're feeling. If you're excited about what you do, people will come and watch you. Whatever you do, you must be excited. My friend Bob Boyd from Columbus, Ohio is a great illustration of what I'm talking about here. I have known Bob since 1972 and what I admire is that he has not lost any of his fire. He has courage. He does not have the highest success rate, but he has courage. Winston Churchill said, "Courage is the capacity to go from failure to failure without losing enthusiasm." I want to warn you when you come out for your dream, you're going to experience failure, and you're going to experience some disappointment.

Bob came to me and said, "Les, I've been working on this idea. All this exposure you got, man, you could make a fortune. This thing is a money machine." I said, "Talk to me, Bob. Talk to me." When he got to explaining it, I said, "Sign me up, Bob. Sign me up." He said, "I want to tell you more about it." I said, "Oh no, I want to play," because he was so excited about it. The fact is that whatever you do, you want to be excited about it. You want to have the kind of excitement that is so contagious people want to be around you. Whenever you talk to people about your particular idea or whatever you're doing, they're watching you and they want to know, do *you* believe it? Are you the kind of person they want to be in business with? If you're not positive, if you're not energetic, if you're not fired up about it, how can you expect anybody else to be? Decide that you have what it takes and that you're going to be fired up about your dream.

When you get ready to work on your goals, you're going to have some problems along the way. Why? It's called life, it comes with the territory. When you get on an airplane, what is the first thing that they tell you to do before you take off? Fasten your seat belts. Because you're going to experience some turbulence before you reach a comfortable altitude. Therefore, it's good to be prepared. Murphy's Law reminds us that "Anything that can go wrong, will go wrong."

I'll never forget when Marlon Brando had a news conference right after his son was adjudicated for allegedly killing his sister's boyfriend. When the news reporters thrust microphones in his face and said, "Mr. Brando, what do you have to say about today's proceedings?" He paused, reflected and said, "The messenger of misery visited my house today." That really hit me hard. I sat down and reflected and thought, "When the messenger of misery visited his house, he passed my house going there." It occurred to me that the messenger of misery is either at your house now or he just left there or he's on the way there.

Why does he have to come? I don't know. Psychologist and Holocaust survivor Viktor Frankl calls it "unavoidable suffering." There's simply too much pain in life to try and duck it. At some point everybody will have their visit. Charles Udall said that, "In life, you will always be faced with a series of God-ordained opportunities brilliantly disguised as problems and challenges." That's where you grow. When you are working on your dream, you're going to have some challenges. In the prosperous years, you put it in your pocket. In the lean years, you put it in your heart. The first time I purchased a home for my mother, I lost it. It was enough to make me want to give up, to say, "Well,

I've lost all of my money in this deal. I guess I just have to settle for just renting now because I made a complete jackass out of myself by not following the details that were necessary to consummate the deal."

Here is the story of what happened. I had a major goal to purchase a home for my mother. There I was, ready to sign the contract and hand over $12,000 of hard-earned money that I had saved to fulfill my childhood dream. The messenger of misery came in the room unbeknownst to me and handled things quietly. My attorney asked, "Do you have a title search on this property that you're purchasing for your mother?" I said, "No, I don't. What's a title search?"

She explained that's when you find out whether or not there are any liens against the property that you might inherit. If there are, then the owner is required to take care of those things. The person that I was buying the property from said, "Excuse me. There are no liens against the property and it will take two or three days to have this done." My attorney said, "I recommend that you do that before signing this contract." The owner, "Listen, I don't want to make this deal right now as it is. I really don't feel good about it because I'm losing money. I'm not using my mind. I'm using my heart. The only reason that I'm selling you this house is I admire the fact that you are adopted and you love your mother and you want to purchase this house for her. I have several other buyers who want to buy this property and will pay me more money. Mister, I spent my time and money coming down here early and I'm losing money providing this deal for you because I think it's a blessing for your mother and for you. Now, if you want to take care of the deal now, let's do it. If not, I'm not going to wait two or three days and lose more money and time from my job and my business." I asked, "Are there any liens whatsoever against the property?" He said, "No." I looked at him and I looked at my attorney and I said, "I believe him." She shook her head. "I would not suggest that you do that." I said, "I believe him. I want to get it now. I'll just take the chance on faith." We signed the contract and I gave him a certified check for $12,000. He looked me in the eyes and he said, "God bless you, young man. God bless you," and embraced me and left.

I felt so good and I went to pick up my mother. We drove to the house and I said, "Mama, this is for you." My mother looked at the house from the car and said, "Oh my. Who would believe, when I adopted you and your brother that this would happen?" I gave her the keys and we went inside. She walked around and said, "Oh, thank you, Lord." With tears running down her face she said, "Who would believe? You, you who caused me so many damn problems." I was such a problem child, but I always had this dream, to get her a house. Abraham Lincoln said, "All that I am and all that I ever hope to be, I owe to my mother."

It was a real big thing in the old neighborhood. Neighbors and friends were astonished and talking about the new house and all came to see her off on moving day. "Bye. Mamie. We're going to miss you. I know you're so proud. You know Mamie adopted the twins. Well, the young one—the bad one, yes, Leslie brought her a home. Oh, wasn't that nice? God's going to bless you, boy. That's so wonderful." We said bye to everybody and took the furniture and belongings to the new house. Then, the messenger of misery started dropping little letters in the mailbox that said "Notification: there is going to be a sheriff sale of the property on the county steps."

There's a lien against the property. I read the letter. I couldn't believe it. It was several weeks after the signing of the contract. I'd forgotten the conversation with the attorney and the former owner. I made a call to him and asked, "What do you mean this property is going up for sheriff sale on the county steps?" The gentleman said, "There's a lien of $25,000 against the property."

"There must be some mistake." I said. "I just purchased this property, and I did not get any loan, sir."

He said, "I'm sorry, sir, but the person that I represent had filed a lien against the property."

I said, "I wasn't the person that got the loan."

He said, "No? Did you get a title search?"

I said, "No, I did not."

"Well, had you had a title search done, you would have known that the money was owed." he replied.

"Well, can I make some arrangements to pay you? What about $1,000 or $2,000 a month." I offered.

He said, "I'm sorry. My client wants all of the money."

"Sir, I can't give you all of it. I bought this house for my mom. I'm adopted. She's in her eighties, and she's got a bad heart and other ailments. This would just be too much of a shock for her. Please, just give me a chance."

"I'm sorry, sir. I'm sorry. We need all of the money."

The messenger of misery had dealt me a hand and I agonized over that. I felt angry. I said, "God, why would you do this to me?"

I'm reminded of the lady who was in the back of an ambulance and she was crying. Her son was shot. She looked at the doctor and said, "Why did this happen to my son?" The doctor replied, "Why not you? Who would you suggest?" See, when I asked life, why does that have to happen to me? "Leslie, why not you? Leslie Calvin Brown, *why not you*?" the messenger of misery said gleefully. I was crying and agonizing over what I was going to do, trying to get money or loans, trying to find out how I could stop the mail to the house that my mother might see. How could I stop people from coming by to look at the property that was going up for sheriff sale? Eventually, I had to tell my mother. At two o'clock in the morning, I went to her and said, "Mama, there's something I've got to tell you. We're going to lose the house." I was kneeling by the bed. She woke up and she said, "I didn't like this house anyway." I said, "What? You got to be kidding." She said, "No, the steps, they hurt my knees—my arthritis—when I'm going up and down the steps. I just said I like the house because of you."

I learned a lot from this experience. I had to learn to let it go. That was one of the challenges I had to go through in order to get a better life for my mother. It was something that I could either allow to devastate me or that I could learn from and to empower me. So I let it go. I can't even remember that seller's name. I concentrated my focus and energy on what was I going to do to earn more money. I got more speaking engagements, more training opportunities. I made more calls and I invested more time and energy to expand my business. I got my mother another home in a better neighborhood and now she's happier than she's ever been. It's called life.

As you say yes to your dreams, decide that you are not going to give up, no matter what. Write down your reasons why it's important to you. Talk to yourself when you find that inner conversation being negative, saying you can't do it. Affirm over and over again, speaking with power, feeling and conviction, "I can do it. I will do it. Yes I can and yes I will," and never give up. As you do that, as you sell yourself on your ability to make it happen, as you continue to plunge forward, as you are relentless in finding ways, becoming more creative and resourceful and determined that you're going to make it happen, you will snatch victory from the jaws of defeat.

The addiction to mediocrity is more pervasive than any drug that we have on the market today. Are you addicted? If you've decided there's greatness within you—and there is whether you believe it or not—if you've decided that you're sick and tired of being sick and tired—and you ought to be—if you've decided to say yes to your dreams, yes to life in spite of the odds, in spite of what other people say, in spite of the fact you can't get other people to approve you, but you've decided to approve yourself, I'd say that's the best decision you can make. You'll be able to look yourself in the mirror one day and say, "I'm glad to be me," and you can now start thinking about what it is you want to do with the rest of the life that you have.

What kind of difference do you want to make on the planet? What is it that you want to bring out here, that you want to share? What ideas do you want to act on so that none of us will ever be the same again, because you showed up on this part of the planet? You've got something special and don't you ever forget.

three

POWERFUL GOALS

Goals are like roadmaps. They give direction to where you want your life journey to take you. Without goals, without a direction, you have nothing to commit yourself to. Look at your life right now. What are some major goals that you can now attach your life to? What kind of work do you have to do to become the kind of person that can reach those goals? How is it that you've got to change? These are the questions to ask yourself right now. What do you want out of life? As you look at your life right now, what is it that will make your life happier, that will give it more meaning? When somebody says, "I'm bored," I say that in order to be bored with life you've got to be boring.

If you're doing the same thing day in and day out, if you don't have any goals for your life, and you're not headed anywhere, you're not stretching, you're not reaching, of course, that's boring because you are boring. What do you want in a career? Maybe you say, I want another career. Why? What do you want that to do for you? How much money do you want to earn? What kind of environment do you want to work in? What is it that you want to do? Do you like working with people or by yourself? What do you want in a relationship? Is that a goal for you? What are you willing to give? What kind of person? What are the qualities of this person? What are you willing to give up? What's your bottom line?

All of these questions are in the areas of goals. What kind of relationship do you want with your friends or your family? Do you want to spend time with them? Are they important enough for you to identify time that you will spend with them and plan some things in advance on what you're going to do with them? One of the goals I had was to become a better father and I thought just paying the bills and buying their clothes and picking them up and taking them places and doing things with them was enough.

But then I discovered that it's one thing to give a check. It's something else to give of yourself. It's something else to learn how to listen. It's something else to go from preaching and teaching and becoming a friend and listening, and sharing and being real, and being honest and being genuine. That's a whole different program because I really didn't know what it took to be a father. It was my goal to do that. I started talking with friends who were good fathers, and who I felt would be good role models for me.

When you look at a goal that you want, a good step is to look at somebody who's doing what you want to do, learn from them, and if you can, develop a relationship with them. I decided that being a speaker alone was not enough. I had to learn how to become a businessman. I had to learn how to work with people and manage people and tasks. I had to start talking to people that I knew were conducting their business in a well-organized way. I wanted to learn from them, so I developed a relationship with them.

In addition to that, I started reading books and learning everything that I possibly could. What are the goals that you have for yourself? Start getting into that mindset. Write those goals down in detail. Don't be vague about it. What are things you need to do daily? What is it that you need to do today? What are your weekly goals, monthly goals, your six-month goals? How do you see yourself a year from now, two years from now, and five years from now? Write it out. Describe what will be there for you. What will be different for you five years from now? How much will you be worth? How much training would you have received? How much time would you have invested in developing yourself?

People ask me, "How can I determine what's going to happen tomorrow?" Tomorrow is based upon what you do today. Right now, you are molding what you will be tomorrow. That's what you're doing. I can tell you what your tomorrow will be like, what it's going to be for you five years from now based upon how much time and energy you spend working on you. If you've got some major goals, then you've got to begin to invest some major time working on you. As entrepreneur and author Jim Rohn said, "A lot of people don't do well simply because they major in minor things."

Hold the completed vision of what it is that you want to do. Look at the picture completed and start breaking it down. What are some of the things that you need to start taking care of right now? Write them down and begin to check them off. As I looked at myself being a speaker, I saw myself on the stage speaking to thousands. Then, I had to come back to where I was today and ask what will it take me to get there? Start hanging around people that are doing what you want to do.

Look at the pros, the masters, the giants, and learn from them. Become a student in life and then start doing little things that you can feel good about.

I started volunteering, speaking for free many times just to get the experience, just to experiment and get my stuff out there, just to get some feedback on how well I was doing, to see whether or not I was on the right track. Once you achieve some small victories, celebrate those victories.

I had a goal of normalizing my weight. I realized that one of my goals should be a health commitment, a commitment to improve my health and stamina. I started managing my food choices. I started doing exercises every day, doing X number of push-ups and sit ups and going for walks. I began to applaud myself and celebrated those victories, and when I got on the scale, I weighed less. You can't do well if you don't feel well. One of the most important goals of all the things you put out is your health. You've got to take care of you, because how well you feel about you helps determine how well you're able to perform in reaching your goal.

Another important thing to understand is that people who make things happen, people who reach their goals have great communication skills. You've got to work with people. You want to be able to communicate with people on all levels. How do you rate yourself as a communicator? Do you work well with people? How's your communication style? Are you open to feedback? Can you give people a reason to want to work with you? Do you inspire people? How do you affect them?

When you talk to people, can you get them to share your vision? Can you motivate them beyond their perceived limits? Can you get them to go with you across the street? This is a different world we're living in today. It's a service-driven economy and the people who have good people skills, who are good communicators are going to come out on top. Communicating does not mean just talking. God has given us two ears and one mouth. That means we've got to learn to do twice as much listening as we do talking. Are you a good listener? Do you ask questions? Do people feel comfortable around you or do you dominate the conversation? Do you have to be right and to have the last word? Look at your skills in these areas. How well you work with people will determine how successful you are in reaching your goals because you can't do it by yourself. You've got to get people to join you. Begin to establish a network of people in your related area. That will enable you to move in the direction you want to go at an accelerated rate.

There is a critical underlying aspect to begin to understand as well. If you decide to deliberately evade your own greatness, if you decide not to work on your goals, I can guarantee you that you're going to be miserable. When you are not living up to your true greatness, you are committing spiritual suicide. People who have goals live longer. More people die after Christmas than any other time of the year. Are you aware of that? This is because they had a goal of living to Christmas. "I just want to see one more Christmas."

What is your dream? What's your goal? Decide that you are going to focus on developing yourself and putting together a strategy to reach your goal. What is it you need to do right now? You've got to put together a game plan. Write it down. What's your plan of action? If you run into some opposition, what will you do? If you run out of money, how are you going to handle that? If this plan of action, this game plan that you have put together, if that strategy doesn't work, what will you do then? You've got to get several strategies, because if it does not work, you want to be able to go back to the huddle and come back out again.

Let's say you had a goal of making $100,000 over the next year. Put together a game plan to identify $300,000 worth of business. Why? Because you want to identify the means to create $300,000 worth of business in the event that some of that business falls through the cracks, in the event that Murphy and the messenger of misery catch you in an alley one day and knock you out. You want to have some other things going for you. If you aim for just the $100,000 and that's the only strategy you put together, I guarantee you won't reach it. You want to identify three times the opportunity beyond the goal you identified for yourself.

Things are more competitive than ever before and you've got to be high energy. You've got to be on fire. You must be excited about what you're doing. The amount of sales that you make, the amount of success that you make, the amount of impact that you make in the industry—if it's writing a book, opening a restaurant, having a grocery store, whatever it is, your success, what you're able to earn, your position in the marketplace—will be directly related to how sold on it you are. How sold are you on it?

You're relentlessly burning the midnight oil, putting in five, ten, fifteen extra hours, whatever is required to make it happen, taking full responsibility for it, because nobody is going to take care of your dream better than you. Nobody is going to care more about your goal than you. I don't care if it's a relative of yours. Nobody is going to do that. They should not. It's yours. Don't expect that. Nobody's going to put in more time than you. As you look at where you want to go, be willing now to come out of yourself, be willing to stretch out, be willing to invest more of you than ever before.

Here's the next quality of people who make their dreams come true. You've got to be unstoppable. That's right. If somebody tells you no, so what? If a door is closed in your face, so what? If things don't work the first time around or the second time around, so what? I wanted to be in a magazine. I called the publisher of that magazine for two years every week. Why? I'm unstoppable. I did get into the magazine. I wanted to be on a national televised program. They said, "You are not an author of a book, are you? You're not a celebrity."

"No, I'm not. But if you give me an opportunity to be on your program, I will become that. I'm a very good guest."

"I'm sorry. We're not in the business of making people celebrities."

"Okay, no problem. But I've got a good message that would be a benefit to your viewers."

"I'm sure you do, sir. Everyone who calls here does. That's the way they feel. Call us when you do something of national significance. Thank you very much."

I didn't go back to that person. I went to someone else. I continued to talk to other people at that particular place until I found someone else that would listen to me. Then I sent her tapes. I called her and developed a relationship with her, and eventually, I was invited to be on that program.

It took me a year-and-a-half to cultivate that relationship, but I was unstoppable. I saw myself on that program. I was willing to initiate the energy, the action. I kept implementing different strategies until I got there. Most people won't do that. They said, "Well, I tried." No, that doesn't get it. If you want to come out here and reach your goals and make your dreams come true, if you want to change careers, you won't do it casually. No. You must put out more energy and more effort than ever before.

When you begin to look at initiating a new strategy for your life, you've got to become unstoppable because there'll be many things to turn you around. You've got to think constantly about *why* you're doing it. What are the rewards? What's there for you across the goal line that you're reaching for, that makes it worthwhile for you? Don't just say, "Well, I want to make more money." After a while, it won't matter. The money won't be enough. You've got to have something else emotionally charging for you, something that's more rewarding for you.

Find some strong and powerful reasons other than just earning a dollar to make it worthwhile for you. I was at a major corporation and was selected to go up for a contract competing against a fellow of Asian descent. We came in on the bus together and when I spoke to him, he didn't answer and I assumed that he couldn't speak English. We two were the finalists and had to present and entertain questions from the panelists. I felt very comfortable with this type of arena. As I've said, I'm a good communicator, and felt that I could prevail.

My co-finalist really surprised me. He was awesome, extremely knowledgeable and articulate and made a brilliant presentation. I won that contract by the skin of my teeth. When I went outside to catch a cab he was still there. I said, "I won that contract. But the next one you might win." He was slightly older than I was and he said something I won't ever forget. "You didn't beat me. What you did was you won scholarship money that I was going to put aside for my granddaughter. You beat her out of that."

"I'm a grandfather too," I replied softly, but his response was something for me to reflect upon. I went in there fighting for a contract, but he went in there with a different commitment. He was thinking about another, future generation. His motivation was entirely different.

What goal do you have? I think we have to begin thinking in terms of generations yet unborn. What kind of stand do you want to take with your life? When you get up in the morning each day and you go to your job or into your business, do you go with a limited vision of how much you're going to earn today to put clothes on your back, food on the table? Or, are you thinking about what kind of legacy you are leaving behind? What kind of preparation? What kind of world are you leaving to future generations? What difference would you have made? What business or service would you have provided that people will have to take note and take their hats off to and say, "Hey, there goes a young lady that really made a difference during our time? There goes a young man that was unstoppable, who identified his goals and against all odds, went all out to make it happen. There's a young lady that refused to be denied that because of her creativeness and resourcefulness. She just refused to give up and she made it happen." What will be said about you? You determine that.

You showed up with the ability to make your dream happen, to reach your goals. You've got the power within you. You have the capacity to take it from a dream to reality. It's going to take more energy. It's going to be very difficult, very challenging. Part of what you must do is initiate action again and again and again. When things don't work out right for you, go back, regroup and come back again and again and again. I remember football coach Jake Gaither from Florida A&M University. Even when they were down by thirty points, Jake Gaither would come on the microphone and he would say in his deep bass voice, "The Rattlers will strike again and again and again and again. We will never give up." That's how you must be with your goals; you must strike again and again and again and never give up. Never, never, never, until you reach your destination. Once you get there, you pat yourself on the back. You celebrate and then you look at where else can I go, what else can I do? This is your universe. You can decide to have another goal to reach for and start working and preparing yourself all over again, reaching and developing and expanding into your greatness, discovering who you are, and unfolding your future and designing and creating what you want it to be. You deserve your goals. It's going to call on everything in you to make it happen.

Another note I want you to keep in mind as you work on your goal is that sometimes you're going to want to give up. That's right. You're going to talk to yourself when life happens and the messenger of misery and Murphy double team you. You want to go back and put the tapes in the garbage can and burn all the motivational books you can find. Why? It's called life. At times you will say, "If I could just find that Les Brown, I'd get him." I can tell you that's a part of it. What do you do then? That's when you get really still within yourself. Listen to that still small voice within you that says, "Hey, even though you might feel like you're alone, even though you might feel that there's just no way you can make it happen, here you are, calling on that inner strength, that something in you that is here to help you."

Eula McClaney wanted a better life for herself. She was working behind a plow at age twenty-six. She got married and had two daughters and went to Pittsburgh with her dream of a better future. Her husband didn't share that dream, but she continued to nag him over and over again and finally, out of exasperation, he said okay. She wanted to go into real estate and he didn't want to do that. She wanted to go to Los Angeles to start all over again. He said, "Why don't you go and take the girls with you? If things work out, fine, if not, at least we won't lose what we have." He was comfortable. He was about maintaining the status quo, but she wanted more. She didn't mind taking some chances.

She went with her two daughters and she started child care in her home and selling slices of sweet potato pie and working part time. It took her two years to save enough down payment on the first piece of property. That was her goal. She wanted to own property. That's all she ever dreamed about. It was like a recurring dream that wouldn't let her rest. Finally, she did it and called her husband. She said, "Come on out. I've got our first piece of property. And something else I want you to realize. Sometimes you're going to be by yourself as I'm out working on my dream." Now her husband said, "I'm not coming," and said he wanted a divorce.

I saw her on *Lifestyles of the Rich and Famous*, and I made it my business to meet her. She told me, "Mr. Brown, I prayed that night. I got on my knees, and said, 'Lord, what can I do to help my husband share my vision of a better future?'" She said the words came to her as clear as day, "Do it yourself." She did it herself.

She told me, "Many times I wanted to give up. Many times, I did not know where I was going to get my next meal from. Many times, I wanted to throw in the towel. I wanted to call my husband and say, 'Baby, you are right. Can we come back home?' many, many times, but during those times, there was something in me that said, 'Don't stop. Don't give up. Just keep on keeping on.' I decided that I wouldn't stop and I made it happen."

She went on to accrue a fortune in real estate in southern California, and lived in an exclusive area in Beverly Hills, becoming active in political fundraising and entertaining society's elites, politicians and celebrities. Before her death she wrote a book called *God, I Listened*, and donated over $30 million to charity.

Eula McClaney didn't stop. Many times when I wanted to give up and wanted to stop I thought about her and how life had dropped her to her knees. Sometimes you're going to have to pray. Sometimes you're going to have to cry. During those moments when you feel powerless in the face of the odds or the opposition—when you run out of money and walk the floor and wonder how you're going to pay your staff or how you're going to pay your bills or how you're going to get a spouse to understand why you've got to do this and they just can't see it—you must talk to yourself and decide. That's why it's important you write those reasons down. Why it's important you're doing it not just for the money, but because it brings meaning to your life. It's important for you to know why you're doing what you're doing, because that's when you're going to have to call on all your resources.

There are many ways to encourage yourself during the turbulent times. I believe that you should identify music that you find uplifting and have it ready to go. Underline quotes in books and have other inspiring thoughts available to read for an energy surge. Identify people that are part of your support committee that you can talk to, who can revive your faith and courage. Have a list of some classes or experiences—like taking a hike—that you can do for inspiration and regrouping. Sometimes you have to take two or three steps back just to go forward again. Sometimes you might have to get a part time job, just to keep things going until you get back on track. It's okay. It's all right.

They say that Walt Disney failed seven times before he reached his goal. It's okay. It's happened to the best of us. It's all right. It won't break you; it only introduces you to yourself. You'll find out that you're more than capable and able to handle it if you don't internalize it. Don't personalize it and realize that it's all a part of the game called life. Don't let anybody turn you around. You deserve your goals. You deserve your dream.

four

A COMMITMENT TO HAPPINESS

Life happens to all of us, and when it does, we have a choice. I think that's the greatest ability that man has above the animals—to choose what he's going to surrender to, or what he's going to embrace. We can choose to be miserable or we can choose to embrace happiness. Begin to realize that whatever we face in life, it is only there for our growth and development, and for enabling us to discover who we truly are. When you focus on problems, you have a state of mind that this is a hassle. This is something that you shouldn't have to deal with when life is just the opposite of that. I believe that life is a classroom and if you view it like that, everything that happens to you, instead of it being a problem, you see it as a challenge. You see it as a project for you to work through. You see it as something there that calls on the very best in you to handle it. You can become a better person because of the challenges as opposed to being intimidated. You look forward to it; you embrace it and you move on to the next level. An airplane cannot fly without the resistance of air. You can't fix lemonade with sugar alone. You can't learn good horsemanship by riding a team horse. There's an old saying, "The harder the battle, the sweeter the victory." When you begin to understand and to know deeply that challenges are things that really make life worthwhile, that stimulate you, that enable you to begin to grow and to expand beyond your wildest imagination, then you begin to realize that without challenges life is fruitless, it's dull, it has no meaning, it has no true value.

Life is like a rollercoaster, sometimes you're up and sometimes you're down. Sometimes things are going well and sometimes they don't go so well. During the down moments, that's when you grow. During the down moments you discover yourself. Life really reveals itself not when things are going well but when things are extremely challenging. That's when you discover your true identity, how boundless and unstoppable you are.

When I was a disc jockey in Columbus, Ohio, there was a listener named Audrey Pilmore who was in a nursing home. She used to call and request certain songs and I would interview her on the air occasionally. I was impressed with Audrey because at age thirty-seven, she had developed muscular sclerosis. She was married, with three children and she had to be confined to a nursing home. Known for her effervescent personality, everybody loved Audrey and she was a blessing to everybody at this nursing home. Her room was constantly full with staff and others seeking her out. This is a woman who never complained, even though she could no longer raise her children.

One day, another listener, Shirley, called and revealed that she was depressed, had undergone a mastectomy, her husband had become distant, and her prospects were grim. She was contemplating taking her life and I asked her, "Could you wait until tomorrow?" She said, "Why?" and I replied, "Because I'd like to introduce you to Audrey Pilmore." She said, after a long pause, "Okay, I will. But I already informed some friends to back me up in the event that this did not work."

I'll never forget the scene when Shirley and I entered her room. Audrey was lying on her back, her body twisted from the disease, and she did not have the capability to fan a fly out of her face. She had no control over her hands, and it was often difficult to even blink her eyes.

Shirley and I walked into her room and said, "Hello, Audrey. How are you doing?" With what strength she had Audrey replied, "I'm doing better than good and better than most." I remember the look on Shirley's face that said, "Why am I here?" But when she looked at Audrey saying, "I'm doing better than good and better than most. How you like me now?" she started thinking within herself. "If this woman can have this kind of determined attitude in spite of her condition, in spite of the fact that she has been confined to this room, to this bed for sixteen years facing death every day, that she can't get up and take herself to the restroom, that she cannot walk down the halls, that she cannot provide for her children—that in spite of all this she can still say that she's doing better than good and better than most—then why am I giving up so easily?"

Shirley looked at Audrey and with tears running down her face said, "I'm so glad, I met you." She said, "Thank you so much. You've been a blessing to me." When we walked out of there, Shirley was a different woman. She had a different walk about her as she realized that there are going to be things that happen to you in life. It's one thing to be happy and have faith when everything's well, when you have your health and your bills are paid and you're not having problems in your relationship and your children are good. But what about when things are stacked against you, and it seems like you cannot make it and you can't see the light at the end of the tunnel, or you don't have your health or you don't have your bills paid? The true challenge is to know that we came with a built-in capacity to handle whatever challenges that life deals out and that we must not take it personally. We do what we must do and keep on keeping on.

People that are working on their dreams and developing themselves have a different kind of walk, a different kind of energy. Their conversations have an upbeat tempo. They have a glow about them. You can tell the difference from people that aren't working on their dream—their movement, their body language, and their voice in conversation. They're often slower, lackluster, and unhopeful. They look at a lot of television, not watching interesting content, just looking. We don't want to be like that. It's better to be actively involved in creating life and making it exciting for you.

Beware of watching and reading too much news lest it make you scared to come out of your house. You've got to keep the little boy and girl alive in you. Most people don't smile. Try it now. Just smile. You look good, you feel better, and people smile in return. Smile and laugh. Learn how to laugh at yourself. Laughing makes you feel glad to be alive.

Cardiologist Robert S. Eliot suffered a massive heart attack and was in the hospital for three months. While there, he reflected on his life after his near-death experience. Neither of his parents had any history of heart failure and lived to be well over eighty. He reflected on the role stress played in his life and how it affects our health. He conducted groundbreaking research into stress and its effects on our health and disease, which he includes in his books, *Is It Worth Dying For?* and *How to Make Stress Work for You—Not Against You.* Among his many memorable quotes are: "In order to live a long life, be happy," and, "Rule number one, don't sweat the small stuff. Rule number two, it's all small stuff." Now that's real.

Harriet Beecher Stowe has an often sited quote for those challenging situations when we feel stuck, "When you get into a tight place and everything goes against you until it seems that you cannot hold on for a minute longer, never give up then, for that is just the place and time that the tide will turn." It could be easier to use difficult times as a signal to turn around; as a stop sign, as opposed to a growth sign. Many will turn around rather than stepping forward. What I've discovered in my own life experience is that at those moments—those times so trying you're at your wits end—that somehow with faith and belief in yourself and your dreams, you can make it through.

Many of us have been in situations like that, where we are overwhelmed with fear. It seemed like the odds were against us, it was impossible to break through, but because we held on, some way, some how, things worked out. How? I don't know. Sometimes I look back and wonder how I got over. I remember the gospel song by James Cleveland that says, "Lord please, help me to hold out until my change come." When you're working on your dream there are going to be times you want to give up. There will be times in life that knock you down and catch you on the blind side and the challenge is to hold on. If you hold on tenaciously, I say the universe is on your side. A way out will appear or someone will step forward and help you somehow.

I still remember this scene from the movie, *The Color Purple*. When young Celie was challenging Albert who told her that she was nothing and always will be nothing and she said, "You might call me ugly, you might call me dumb, you might call me stupid, and I might not be able to talk, but I'm still here. I'm still here." We can say that about ourselves. My bills might not be paid. You might have divorced me. Things aren't what I want them to be. My life might be in shambles right now, but in spite of all of that, I'm still here. I still have some work to do. My work on this plane is not through yet. As long as I'm here, I can make a difference. As long as I'm here, I can become an active force to turn things around; this has not come to stay.

Trouble does not last always. This too shall pass. Many times, when things happen to us and we're in the throes of it, we believe that it's going to be that way forever. It's never like that. At some point in time, it's going to leave. This too shall pass. When you know that you can operate with a sense of expectancy, you expect things to get better. When you are dealing with a particular challenge, you handle the challenge. While you're in the challenging situation, you continue to make things happen. You continue to move. You don't stop. You don't start feeling sorry for yourself. You don't call people and talk about how bad things are for you. Watch the language, watch the conversation that you have because whatever you focus on, whatever you talk about constantly, that's what you're going to produce and expand and multiply in your life experience.

I tell people watch what they say, because words are clothed with energy and they began to materialize. Start watching your inner conversations and pay attention to what you're saying. If you're going through some challenges, instead of, "I'm broke," say, "I'm overcoming a cash flow problem." Rather than, "I'm sick," try, "I'm overcoming a physical challenge. Every day in every way, I'm getting better and better." If you just do those two things, watch your inner conversations and reframe what you're saying about yourself, your world, your affairs, your circumstances, you will find this too shall pass.

If you can't say something good, don't say anything at all. Don't allow people to encourage you to chime into the negative conversations of the world. If you listen to what everybody else is saying, if you judge according to appearances, then you will find yourself constantly being negative. Of course we all want to know how things are going to get better. How? I don't know and I don't have to know. I just have a feeling that everything is going to be all right. Why? What proof do you have? I don't have to produce any proof. All I need to do is to know it, to expect it, and to keep on doing what I can, where I am with what I've got right now, living in the moment, and realizing that this too shall pass. Part of what we need to do is allow our inner child to activate itself to do certain things.

When I'm working with various groups, doing workshops or seminars, I have people get physically involved in certain gestures or little rituals. One is to repeat an affirmation out loud whenever you can, wherever you are. I don't care what you're doing. You might be driving along the highway or working around the house, but say this and say it strong,

I throw away negative thoughts.

I throw away guilt.

I throw away negative people, and all of the unnecessary
    baggage that's been holding me back.

We must begin to find little ways to make ourselves peaceful, to cultivate happiness. Here's another affirmation I'd like you to say out loud right now:

I bring in faith.

I bring in peace of mind.

I bring in good relationships.

I bring in good health.

I bring in love.

I bring in money.

I bring in every good thing in the universe that you live in.

Always remember that in spite of how bad things might appear to be, you're still here, you still are a worthwhile person and you have so much to be thankful for.

If you go through life holding grudges, wanting to get even or get revenge, you will find out that the person holding the hatred, the anger and the resentment is doing more damage to themselves than the person they aimed that hatred or anger at. The best way to deal with the challenge of overcoming any kind of hot feelings that you might have about someone, regardless of what they have done to you is to ask yourself the question, how does this help me? Is it something that I need to hold on to? Is it helping me to grow and to move into the future? Is it weighing me down? How do I feel inside myself when I'm holding these negative feelings toward this person?

In my particular case, for a long time I hated my mother and father because I never knew them. I was living with the feeling that they gave me away. I never saw or knew them, so I didn't have any way to visualize a target for my hatred. I was reading the poet Kahlil Gibran and his thoughts about children, "They come through you but not from you." That particular line just liberated me. In conjunction with the reality that I was adopted, and chosen with love, I was free from my years of hatred. I said, "Wait a minute. I'm a child of the universe. I came through somebody, but I came from the universe." I realized it really did not matter who got together to produce my brother and me. I spent a long time wondering what my father looked like, what my mother looked like, what kind of people they were. Did I have any other brothers and sisters?

I conducted some seminars with a medical professional who was obsessed with trying to find his parents. We had something in common, both being adopted. He was a part of a group that helps people find their biological parents. At one point he said, "Man, your life is not complete until you find your parents." I was dubious as my life was going well and for many years. He did help another friend of mine find his father. He went to the house, and knocked on the door. There he is looking like his father's identical twin and he said, "Hi, I'm your Son." The father slammed the door in his face saying, "I don't have a son." I'll never forget the look on my friend's face when he came down the steps. He said, "I wished I had never found him. At least I would not have to live with the rejection that even now, he doesn't want me." Of course all stories are unique and many reunions of adoptees and birthparents work out very well. For me, in my particular situation, I say that whoever my parents are, bless them. For my wonderful mother Mrs. Mamie Brown, bless them. You have to deal with the hand you've got, and going through life carrying the luggage of anger and resentment, regret and guilt, is really weighing you down.

I decided, since I can decide, that I don't want to carry this luggage with me. It's not helping me to grow mentally, emotionally and spiritually. It doesn't matter. The only value that it has, the only meaning that it has, is that which I give it. That might sound simple but I tell you this, we do have the power to choose who we are going to serve, our negative law in nature or our higher self. If you feel that being angry, having resentment and guilt works for you, then go on with it. If you want to be free and you have the capacity to be free, you can free yourself. Your future is open, and the possibilities are unlimited. If that glass is empty, you can fill it with milk. You can fill it with water. You can fill it with wine. You can fill your life with anger and regret and resentment, or you can decide right now, wherever you are, to fill your life with love, with forgiveness, with compassion, and with understanding. You can choose to let what happened make you bitter or make you better. That choice is in your hands. As we begin to move into the future and begin to know that we hold that kind of power, then we can choose to embrace happiness, we can choose to be or not to be. That is the question—to be in charge of your feelings, your emotions and your thoughts, or not to be in charge, to surrender to the negative mindset of the world.

Choose to stand strong within yourself. Say, "I choose to be happy. I deserve to be happy." It really doesn't matter what happens to me. As Elsie Robinson said, "Things may happen around you and things may happen to you, but the only things that really count are the things that happen in you and we control that."

five

THE RIGHT PEOPLE

I read an article once about *The Right Ingredient*. I think that anybody who has ever done anything in life of any special significance has had the right ingredients. They had some people there who had all of those streams where they were weak, and were able to compliment them. When you look at major corporations, there's always a person behind the scene, that second-in-command person, that can make all of the difference, the difference between being successful and failing. I think it's very important that you can give yourself what I call a "home court advantage" in life. Sports studies indicate that when a team is on the road, they usually lose more than when they are at home. They win at home because they have people there rooting for them. They're more confident, they feel more comfortable in their territory—in their home court—and because they have people saying, "Hey, you can do it."

Even when they are down by points, those people are cheering them on. It gives them a certain adrenaline flow. It gives them a certain level of competency or extra thrust where they can go beyond where they ordinarily would. It's very important that you see the value of aligning yourself with what I call OQP, "only quality people." Look at people around you or people that are doing what you want to do, and select people who can enhance, enrich, and empower you, people who will enable you to transcend yourself by assembling a team that has been handpicked by you. OQP are people that can be an asset to you.

You can give yourself an extra winner's edge by assembling a team that can complement you and strengthen you where you're weak, and enable you to go across the finish line or reach the goals that you want to reach at a much faster rate. It's important when people are with you, that they see where you're going. Not only must they share your vision, but they must see how they fit in the vision. In order to manifest your dream and to produce the results that you want, it's going to take a lot of energy. You want people who will stand with you—you cannot do it by yourself. We win with people.

It has been said that one negative comment is sixteen times more powerful than a positive comment. When that comment comes from someone that you love, that you respect, or from someone who should be there for you, someone who should be cheering you on, it hurts very much. When a spouse or family member says to you, "you can't do it," that hurts worse than coming from somebody who you don't know. Criticisms are very powerful. I don't know anything that can destroy your desire, your dream, or your passion faster. I know a lot of people never ever acted on their dreams or their ideas because people around them— people they respected or looked up to—said, "I don't think you should do that, or I don't see that for you, or I don't think you should try and get involved in that area. You're not good enough."

They did not venture out on their ideas because someone they highly respected did not approve of the idea. They decided they couldn't do it, because they were seeking the approval of people they cared about. I think that it's important that you surround yourself with people who are positive, who can see the possibilities for you, who will not be yes people for you and just agree with you all the time, but at least have a sense of adventure and say, "Why not? Go take it on."

I have in my life, some trusted critics, people who will tell me stuff that I *need* to hear, not only what I *want* to hear.

The quality circle of people that you have with you must include people who are able to challenge you, who help you stretch mentally, intellectually, personally and spiritually. These are not "yes-men," who just go along with you. These are the people who will tell you things you can't get anywhere else. They care about you. It can be uncomfortable and doesn't always feel good to hear constructive criticism. I have one person, Mike, who tells me things I don't like hearing at all. I hate being on the hot seat, but I cannot grow without that. He and the other people in my life who care about me might tell me things I disagree with. But I know they're giving it to me straight. They're telling me about my blind spots. These are things I have to take into consideration.

Ultimately, it's always my decision. I can still decide to take the information and act on it, or I can just ignore it and say, "Hey, I got that. I know how you feel. I appreciate you telling me and I'm going to do it this way. This is the way I see it and what I'm going to do."

In the end *you* have to make the decision. You don't want to say, "Well, if I had just listened to my first mind." Listen to your people and their feedback and you decide. Many times I did not listen to my first mind.

I followed other people's advice because I thought they knew what they were talking about and they were right. Then there were times I said, "I've got to do this because I just feel it in my gut. I can't explain it. I can't justify it, but there's something that tells me to do this." I've been right sometimes, and I've been wrong. I was willing to take the chance because I had my quality circle of support to help when needed.

If you decided you're not going to allow your fears to stop you, what would your life be like? What would your future be like if you decided to want that which you desire so strongly, that it helps you past your fears? You experience the fear, and as the book title by Susan Jeffers says, *"Feel the Fear and Do It Anyway."* All of us who had been paralyzed by fear have the capacity to resurrect ourselves and our dreams. Is it easy? No. It's not easy. Can I do it? Yes. What's one of the ways to get started? Some of us need people to hold our hands. Sometimes you need that. None of us can do everything by ourselves.

My friend who fears sailing is afraid of the water. I suggested swimming lessons. She needs some coaching. You can do it step by step. She can take some classes and learn how to swim. Then practice and improve, and then she can go into the deep end of the pool, and finally, sailing. She just needs some coaching. Whatever you're dealing with, get some coaching.

Sometimes we need somebody to help us out, show us the steps, let us practice and then set sail.

Be willing to say, "I don't know." Be willing to reach out. Be willing to get some assistance to take you to the next level. As Joe Frazier said, "All of us are like the blind man at some point in our life standing on the corner, waiting for somebody to lead us across." All of us, at some point in our lives, need help, need someone to reach out to us with the thought, the lifeline, to help us across some treacherous waters that we couldn't navigate by ourselves. None of us do it by ourselves. We grow from the people who enrich our lives personally, professionally, mentally and spiritually and we don't grow in a vacuum.

Dr. Sidney Simon, author of *Negative Criticism,* talked about the qualities of the people in your life and said there are two kinds of people. He said there are "toxic" people and there are "nourishing" people. Nourishing people inspire you. They bring out the very best in you like my mentor, Mr. Leroy Washington. He was a teacher who lit up the room when he entered as every one of his students felt special, felt inspired, felt that they could win any debate, ace any role in any play, ace any test, because he thought they could.

What about the toxic people? I call these people "energy drainers." These are people who can demoralize the most positive person and cause them to fall way below their potential. As Dr. Johnnie Colemon said, "If you can't bring the people up in your life, for God's sake, don't let them bring you down." It takes a lot of energy to reach your goals. Toxic people drain you mentally, emotionally, physically and spiritually. They are negative, complaining and critical. They are constantly pointing out your shortcomings, complaining but never offering solutions and arguing about everyone and everything. When people like this are in the workplace, productivity drops. I once had a workplace situation where I removed one toxic person and the entire atmosphere changed immediately, even the air was easier to breathe. There are some people that are not good for your health or your blood pressure and definitely not good for your disposition.

There are some people who bring out the worst in you and I think you should just avoid those people at all cost. I have a friend who changes his whole personality when he is around a certain group of people. He starts using profanity, drinking and experimenting with drugs. Put him in another setting and he's a totally different person. These people that bring out the worst in him are people he really should avoid. Just leave them alone. Don't try and argue with them. Don't try and convert them, just leave them be. There are some people who are good for you, who bring out the best in you. They inspire you. They make you feel good about yourself. They complement you. They empower you; enable you to see all kinds of possibilities for yourself. Make a conscious effort to be around those people.

I went to Booker T. Washington High School with Willie Covington and Larry Little, both football players on our school team. Covington was the more talented player, faster, stronger, more agile with more ability. The primary difference between the two is significant. Larry used to practice every day. He would run in the park every day. He was slower and people use to tease him but he didn't care. He wanted to become a football player. That was his mission and his destiny. Covington didn't have the same discipline and he ran around with the guys who liked to steal cars and go for joy rides. He was finally arrested for stealing a car and incarcerated. Larry went off to Bethune-Cookman College, and then became an all-pro offensive guard with the Miami Dolphins and went on to win the Super Bowl twice.

I was on a cross country tour and had a speaking engagement at a prison in Florida. They said there's somebody here who knows you. Sure enough, it was Willie Covington. He came up from the kitchen, still muscular and strong, same gregarious personality as ever. He had spent the best of his years behind bars and eventually died of a heart attack. Two men, both talented, one more gifted than the other. I once wrote, "Many a flower has bloomed unceasingly and wasted sweetness upon the cold desert air." The world never had the chance to see the talents, the ability, and the gift of Covington, because he was not willing to leave the toxic negative people that caused him to forfeit his dream.

Covington was a good person, but he ran with the wrong crowd. I've seen that happen to many young people and also many adults. I do training in prisons and I once did an extensive interview with young men and women who were there because of drugs. I asked, "Where were you? What was going on the first time that you committed your crime, or the first time you experimented with drugs?" All of them said without exception, "I was with a friend." I was with a friend. I say to parents constantly that the person that will induce your kids to use drugs is not some stranger lurking in the dark with shades on, who jumps out and says, "Here, try this. It'll make you feel good."

The person that our children are most vulnerable to is the person that they trust, that they like, that they want to be accepted by, that they run with all the time—a friend. A close friend will say, "Hey, come on, I did it. Oh, you scared? I thought you were a hip. Come on, try it." That friend, that's the one that causes many of us to derail our dream. You've got to be very selective of your friends. My mother used to say, "Birds of a feather flock together." If you run with losers, you will end up a loser. That is true for adults as well as young people. It's very important for you to look at yourself and evaluate your relationships. There are some that start out positively, and suddenly, become toxic, they become very negative, and those people are no longer good for you.

Evaluate the people in your life at different stages of your life and ask yourself, "Is this relationship giving me what I want? Is it good for me? What kind of person am I becoming because of this relationship?" If you see that the relationship has gone downhill or is not what it used to be, it's not a plus in your life. In fact, it's now a minus—it's a liability. Now you have to make a decision. Can we work this out? What do we need to do to get back on track? If it cannot be worked out, then you've got to part company. You have to say, "This is not working." I had a friend and we were doing well together. He started drinking and the drinking became a problem.

One of the best employees I had started coming to work late. He wasn't taking care of business as he should. I was getting all kinds of complaints from my customers. I said, "What is it we could do to help correct this problem? Is there anything I can do? Do you need to be picked up so you can get here on time? What assistance can I provide?" We couldn't come up with anything. He said, "Well, it's me. I've got some problems I'm trying to work out." I wanted to give him all the assistance I could, and gave him a deadline to handle it.

He didn't handle it and we had to part ways. He was one of the best people I had, but that positive relationship began to turn toxic. Sometimes that happens. If it turns out that this person is no longer good for you, or you're no longer good for them, acknowledge that and go your separate ways. It doesn't have to be ugly. It can be positive. "Look here, we're growing in different directions. Our values have changed. Our goals and objectives have changed. Maybe we need to just shake hands and leave now." You don't have to leave on a negative note. There does not have to be a big fight.

My friend Pat has a dramatic and very real story of what a negative person can do. Pat was living with a friend who had an alcohol and drug problem and was very argumentative. This person was hell to deal with, just miserable, complaining and critical. They would have arguments all of the time, about anything. One day while Pat was at work, her coworkers noticed that she walked with a slight limp. As it became worse and more noticeable they asked her about it. She hadn't noticed but did admit she was feeling off physically so she went to the doctor. Sure enough, one leg was shorter than the other. The doctor didn't know the cause and didn't know of any treatments.

Pat still had the same home situation, arguing day in and day out. One day out of exasperation she finally said, "You've got to go, I've got to go. I'm tired of you and I'm tired of this situation. I'm tired of going through physical changes. It's just too stressful." Pat told her to go and her friend moved out. A few weeks later she was walking normally. We'll say the moral of this story is get negative people out of your life, or you run the risk of one of your legs growing up on you.

When I'm working with students or with inmates in the various volunteer programs that we have, one exercise we do is taking inventory. I'm asking you to do the same thing. Make a list of the people that you communicate with most. It might be relatives, people you work with, friends, a spouse, or siblings. Make a list of the people that you are in the most contact with. After you do that, next to each name on your list answer this question: What kind of person am I becoming because of this relationship?

Look at the people in your life. Do they enhance you personally, spiritually, intellectually, and professionally? Look at what kind of impact they're having. If you review people at different points in your life you may discover that there are some people that are not good for you. There are some people you may need to decrease your exposure to. They are not good for your life. In fact, they will sabotage your life.

Look at these people on your list and say their names. If the energy level goes up, put a check by their name. When I look at the lives of the great people I've known or have read about, they have all had someone that they pointed to and could say, "Because of this person, I'm a different person. Because of this person, my life will never be the same again." As I look at my life I can point to my mother; I can point to my high school teacher, Mr. Leroy Washington; I can point to Mike Williams, my personal coach and mentor.

At the end of the year, many stores have clearance sales, and before that, many do inventory to check out what they have on the shelf. The merchandise that's collecting the most dust that was not moving in spite of big promotions will certainly not be brought back next year. But the merchandise most popular with consumers, that sold the most, this will be stocked up.

One of the best things that we can ever do for our lives is to be constantly seeking and nurturing relationships with people that will help us stretch, people that will call forth the best and the highest in us. Take a look at the people that we allow in our lives to love us, and that we love, the people that bring out the very best in us, the people that we know are good for us. It is through people that you will discover things *about* yourself that you can never discover *by* yourself. As you look toward the goals you want to achieve, align yourself strategically with people who enrich you, who enhance you, who will enable you to reach beyond your present vision of yourself and to transcend yourself. These are the people who will enable you to manifest the greatness that you have within you, the best that you have to offer the universe.

six

WHATEVER IT TAKES

Most of us go through life pretending. Pretending that we're satisfied where we are, pretending that everything is okay, pretending that we don't have any special goals or ambitions or desires—when really deep down inside, we do really want more. If you look at our behavior, if you judge us based upon what we do, that will really tell you the true stories—you have to judge a tree by the fruit it bears not the fruit that it talks about. A lot of people pretend that they want more out of life, but if you watch their actions they will tell you something else. I used to pretend that I wanted to lose weight. How could you tell I was pretending? Watch me when I have a piece of sweet potato pie.

Get me near some peanuts or potato chips and watch what I do. If you just watch what I eat that would tell you what I'm seriously committed to. People will tell you, "One day I want to have a restaurant." But they're pretending they want to go into business for themselves. How can you tell they're not serious? Let's watch their actions, watch what they're doing. The proof is in the pudding. If you want to do something, if you thought about something you want to do, take it head on. Decide that you are going to start looking at it, researching it. Start tackling it, start becoming involved in whatever is needed to explore the possibilities. You must begin to learn all you can about it.

Decide that you're going to face whatever shortcomings you have and strengthen yourself there. You're going to get whatever training is required and you're going to get started right now. George Washington Carver would say. "Do what you can, where you are with what you have and never be satisfied." Yes, don't get satisfied with yourself. Always know that wherever you are, you can enjoy more, that you deserve more. Most people know they deserve more yet they go through life quietly and will safely tiptoe into an early grave. Find out what it is you want, and go after it as if your life depends on it. Why? Because it does. People who have found their passion, people who have found the things that they love, people who have found the things that they can pour their lives into—those people live longer.

I was in New York to do a seminar at Reverend Johnny Youngblood's church. I asked, "How is it that you were able to get all of the various community and religious groups together to build this affordable housing for more than 2,000 formerly homeless residents? How were you able to take on this responsibility? Wasn't it overwhelming?" He said, "The kind of work I do, it's in me. I've got to live what's in me." I think that's everybody's desire in life, to live what's in you. Life is just too short and unpredictable. But what do we say instead, "Well, there's always tomorrow."

No. There are no guarantees you're going to show up tomorrow. A lot of people who were here yesterday are not here today. There are a lot of opportunities that were around yesterday and they're not here today. You can wait but remember what Abraham Lincoln said, "Things may come to those who wait, but only the things left by those who hustle." Who wants to go through life picking up leftovers? Let's see what they left back here for me? No, absolutely not. You deserve much more than that.

Look for ways to increase your value in life. If you're working on a job, find ways in which you can make yourself indispensable. When I became involved in broadcasting, I not only became a top-rated disc jockey, I learned everything I could about production, how to write and produce commercials, an how to edit. I learned everything I could about being the news director and the program director, and eventually I became the manager of station operations. Learn how to do more things and to do them more effectively. As we begin to move toward optimizing the efficiency of our operations, we can increase our profit margins as well as improving the quality of the service we want to provide for the American public, or for the world as we are now in a global economy.

In order to do that, it's important that you learn everything you can about what you're doing, because most people won't do that. If you look at life as a race or as a competition, understand that what you are really doing is competing with yourself. If you decide to work really hard at what you do, to master it, you'll beat 50% of the others, because 50% will just not work as hard. I was at a function the other day. After speaking, some young fellows approached me to say they were interested in becoming professional speakers. Later that evening, they were saying, "Hey, let's go out and have a good time tonight." I admit that when I was their age, I wanted to have a good time, too. However I was more committed to disciplining myself, to perfecting my craft, to learning everything I could. When I admired a speaker or presenter at a seminar, I would seek them out. I wanted to find out everything that I could, what books they were reading, who influenced their thinking. I wanted access to their information, to their knowledge, so that I could develop in their field. These young fellows said they wanted to grow, but only after they partied and had a good time. In my option, they're not really working on manifesting greatness.

What they really want is to just get into the profession. They want to show up; they're not coming to making a dramatic difference or take the profession to another level. They just want to be in the game, but not to make any true difference in the game. I say that whatever you do, decide not to just show up, but ask what it is that you can bring. What is it that you could do, that as a result of being involved in this arena it will never be the same again? How can you have the same impact in this area as Mozart had on music, as Larry Bird has had on basketball, as Pavarotti has had in music?

As we begin to look at ourselves, let's decide that we have something unique that we showed up with, that nobody can bring this out here like we can. What is it that you must do to discover, to develop and to tap that greatness, that uniqueness that you were born with? It takes practice. A lot of people believe that practice makes perfect. No, it does not. Practice makes improvement as Ed Foreman has said so many times at the Executive Development Systems training sessions. The more you do, the more you realize you can do. The better you are, the more you realize how much better you can become. People who expect to make it are the people who become successful in life.

You don't have to tell a student who expects to graduate to do their homework, to go to the library, to go to class. You don't have to tell an athlete who expects to be great to practice, to get his rest, or not to smoke or drink. You don't have to roll an athlete who expects to be great out of bed in the morning. They do that automatically, that expectation shows up in their behavior. A person who wants to be successful in business, who expects to be a top salesperson, doesn't need to be told to do certain things—to follow up and follow through, to have an attention to detail. They do that automatically, it comes with the territory.

You know the competition is stiff, so before you step out into the arena you do your homework, you do your research. You get more than enough information so that you will have the tools, the knowledge, and the information to be properly armed to take on any competitors. You've been thorough in your work and have left no stone unturned. We must be willing to provide a quality of service beyond the expectations of our clients. Doing that requires a great deal of preparation, research, attention to detail and listening, asking questions and caring enough to provide the very best that you can for them.

Civil rights leader Whitney Young said, "It's better to be prepared for an opportunity and not have one than to have an opportunity and not be prepared." I did not wait until I had Fortune 500 clients in order to develop a Fortune 500 professional approach. I knew that at some point in time, I was going to be up there with the big guys. Early on I had my eye on the big picture and started working, developing myself, paying attention to the details that would enable me to provide a quality presentation for that audience. This approach accelerated my growth and my explosion into the speaking industry.

This can apply to anybody, whatever you're doing. I don't care if you're involved in sales or marketing, management, operations, or accounting. If you decide you have a larger vision of where you want to go, see yourself there, and ask yourself the question, "What kind of Chief Executive Officer must I become? What kind of salesperson? What kind of marketing person? What type of manager? What type of supervisor must I become? What is it that I need to change about me? What areas of my skills, my leadership potential do I need to work on, to strengthen? What knowledge or training do I need right now that I don't have? What kind of habits do I need to change? How can I begin to transcend myself and develop the kind of conscious-ness that will enable me to produce the results that I want in my life?"

In life you don't get what you want, you get what you are, what you subconsciously believe that you deserve. As you look at where you want to go, you are constantly working to become that kind of person, that kind of manager, deliberately developing yourself to have that kind of consciousness to create what you want in your life. Another good feature is to set high standards for what you do. It's surprising how many people don't set high standards.

I once pulled into a service station and there were two cars in front of me and two cars behind. The ser-vice station attendant was taking care of a credit card transaction which was taking longer to handle. If this guy had set some standards for himself he might have said when cars are backed up I'm going to make eye contact with each driver, smile and say, "Listen, we're busy right now as you can see. I'll be right with you. Please don't leave because I want your business. Be right with you." That gesture would have made all the difference in the world and the wait would not have been so long. But eventually the other drivers and I got fed up and left because he never looked at us. He never acknowledged us and people want to be acknowledged.

People want to know that you see them, that they are not invisible, that you want their business, that you value them. This worker did not have that kind of commitment nor did the owners of that service station.

Another time I had a completely different experience at a hotel. Usually when you leave a hotel in the morning, you pass the people that handle the changing of the linens and they never speak to you. This particular hotel had some high standards. As I was walking down the hall, each person there to clean the rooms made eye contact and said, "Good morning. How are you? Did you enjoy your stay here? I'm so glad. Do come back again. We're going to miss you." Now that was a good feeling. Someone in management said, "When people leave this hotel, we want them to leave on a good note."

In the real estate industry I have an agent who is not an effervescent personality, but she sells millions of dollars of real estate each year. I asked her what the key to her success was. She said she goes all out to let her clients know that she cares about them, that making money is secondary. Her philosophy is if you put the customer first, you'll never come in second. She has high standards on letting her customers know that she cares about them. As a result, 99% of all of her business is repeat business or referral business, because people spread the word. She has a reputation for taking care of you.

Those things that come from setting high standards for what you do can make all the difference in your life. Mastering what you do, practicing, developing the technical knowledge, having high standards for taking care of what you do and how it looks, the quality and elegance in which you bring the service or product out here all help you get to the next level. Just go at it and say, "I'm going to do this unlike anybody has ever done this before on the planet. When folks see me or see my work or my product, they're going to go out talking about it."

Once you master what you do and continuously work at achieving that level of mastery, the next thing is that you have got to go at it massively. You want everybody to know that you do it. There's an old Chinese saying, "If you throw enough rice on the wall, some of it will stick." I threw a whole lot of rice. I decided that I wanted to do far more than the average person. I made 200 calls a day, I would talk to anybody who got within three feet of me about my business and what I was doing because I feel that everybody is a potential client.

I wanted everybody talking and I started spreading seeds like Johnny Appleseed everywhere I would go. The name of the game is TTP—Talk to People. If that doesn't work, TTMP—Talk to More People. Eventually, when you plant all of these seeds you will be surprised when they start coming in. Once they start, they start coming from everywhere. It might take a week, or three months, or six months, or a year. Three years ago I gave my card to someone. He just ran across it and called, "I remember meeting you three years ago, and I was intending to get back to you. I just found your card. I would like to do some business with you."

I sent out promo tapes, and one was just lying on this man's desk. His visitor looked at it and said, "That sounds like it's for me. How can I get in touch with him?" Don't be afraid to promote yourself, it's part of believing in yourself and your dream. You've got to see what you do—your business, your service, your product or the knowledge that you have—you've got to see it as your life's mission. When you go out as a missionary, as a movement, as a crusade, the possibilities are just unlimited.

You will begin to reap incredible rewards from your promotional efforts because at some point, when you put enough stuff out there it's going to come back. Many people lay back and wait for their ship to come in, but I think you need to swim out to that ship and pull it in. I think that people who are able to make a difference in life are people who have developed themselves in terms of their consciousness to begin to move forward. What do I mean by consciousness? Consciousness is a collection of your thoughts, feelings, perceptions and impressions you can mobilize to move toward your dream. Activate your consciousness to help you take the plunge, to get out there, to get into the flow, and move yourself and your dream forward.

When you decide to start making things happen you will unleash even more energy to drive yourself toward your goals. It may seem safer to wait, to say, "I'm going to do it when I pay all my bills. I'm going to do it when the market changes. I'm going to do it when things get better. I'm going to do it after I resolve this issue over here." Things will never be 100 percent ideal. You've just got to decide to act now. "I'm going to make my move now and so be it. If it works out, fine."

Most people take their ideas to their graves, not wanting to make any mistakes, not wanting to fail, not wanting to step on anybody's toes, not wanting to hurt anybody's feelings, wanting to be known as the nice guy or nice lady, not wanting to be perceived as being pushy. They go to their graves with all of their music in them, because they weren't willing to act. They weren't willing to step into the arena. They weren't willing to take care of business. You've got to decide within yourself—come what may, let the chips fall where they will, I'm going into action. I'm going to do something and I'm going to do it now. So what if I make some mistakes. If I get blown out, at least, at least I'll be able to stand up and say, "I gave it my best shot."

Most people don't do that, they never take their best swing. Most people never even discover their true talents and abilities because they go through life holding back.

I remember I was pulling out of my driveway one day. As I mashed down on the accelerator, the car was sluggish and it did not move and I mashed down harder and it still was sluggish. Suddenly I realized I had on my emergency brakes. Once I released them the car went, boom, unencumbered. Many of us never act because we put on our emergency brakes—sometimes called "procrastination" or "is it safe?" or "what will people say?" or "I don't have any money," or "I would if I could."

I say get your butt out of the way and decide that you're going to take care of business right now. It's hard and I'm going to do it. It's challenging, yes, and I'm going to make it happen. I don't have the money and I'm going to find a way to get it. They've said no. Okay. I'm coming back until I find a yes. I feel that's the kind of spirit you must have—deciding to act and going into action right now, right where you are. Refuse to allow anything to discourage you from jumping out into the arena called life.

seven

BECOME A POWERFUL PERSON

Each of us must model integrity, and the making and keeping of our commitments. As we strive toward our goals these are among the basic principles for enriching our lives and those around us. Powerful people can be role models for all of us. It takes courage to model integrity, to live with the courage of your convictions. It takes a great deal of heart to transform yourself and to take a stand that's unpopular. There is an often repeated quote by Herbert Bayard Swope that says, "I can't give you a sure-fire secret for success, but I can give you a formula for failure: try to please everybody all the time." Powerful people have realized that they're not consensus takers and have gathered the courage to move toward what they believe are the right goals.

Martin Luther King, Jr. said, "Cowardice asks the question, is it safe? Expediency asks the question, is it politic? Vanity asks the question is it popular? But conscience asks the question, is it right? And there comes a time when one must take a position that is neither safe, nor politic, nor popular, but one must take it because it is right."

Even though people might not like you for the stand that you take, they will respect you for that stand. When I was serving in the Ohio State Legislature, one of the things I admired most about the Speaker of the House was that even when you disagreed with him on an issue that was very close to him, he respected you because you were consistent. He recognized your strong feelings regarding your position and respected your taking a stand for them. He might want your vote very much, but he respected people who did not compromise their positions—who took that stand because that's what they felt within their heart. You have the capacity to do that, to be powerful in all of the relationships in your life, be it in the work environment or in your family.

When I had to make a decision regarding my son, I remembered reading something that Betty Davis said, "In order to be a very good parent, you've got to be willing to be comfortable with your children hating your guts." If we need our children to love us all the time, we make concessions we ordinarily would not make. In many cases, we are doing them a disservice because we're not making the kind of firm, strong, courageous decisions that will ultimately help them have the right direction they need in order to manifest their own inherent greatness.

When we ask how can I become a more powerful person, one of the most fundamental things is to have the courage to be true to yourself. Find the courage to do that which is right because it is the right thing to do, not because everybody else is going to agree with you or like you. Everybody is not going to like you. In fact, even if you could go along with everybody, there are people who will dislike you for doing that, saying that you have no integrity; that you're a yes person who goes along with anything.

In order to become more effective in relationships, integrity is very important. You've got to be honest. Winston Churchill said, "The truth is incontrovertible. Malice may attack it, ignorance may deride it, but in the end, there it is." Another quote I like is from Herbert Agar, "The truth that will set people free and enable them to do what they want to do is the truth that most people prefer not to hear." Powerful people will often take stands that are unpopular and they hold their ground. These are times that we all have to make strong decisions in our lives. Making a decision to be honest with yourself and to admit you're not getting what you want from your job is a big step. Being honest and acknowledging that you're not performing up to your potential is paramount. Making the decision to make a change as opposed to settling, "Well, I'm getting good benefits here. I'm just ten years away from retirement, so I'm going to ride it on out." There's no guarantee that you're going to be here ten years from now. If you decide to continue this ride called "being mediocre," by scaling your dreams down or denying yourself the opportunity to move on, you're doing yourself a tremendous disservice as well as the people that you're working for.

Deciding to be a powerful person means deciding to act and to act from a sense of integrity and courage. We used to say this on-air constantly when I was a disc jockey, "Stand up for what you believe in because you can fall for anything." People who are powerful are people who have found something that they can pour themselves into completely.

There are many reasons I like to use the comeback of boxer George Foreman to illustrate how powerful people operate in the world. Soon after losing the World Heavyweight title to Muhammed Ali, George Foreman retired from boxing, became an ordained minister and devoted himself to his family, his church and a youth center that still bears his name. When he decided to make a comeback after ten years away from boxing it surprised everyone, and many thought it was a big mistake. He said he wanted to prove that age was not a barrier to achieving your goals. After winning matches and regaining his fitness he decided that he was going to fight Evander Holyfield for the heavyweight championship of the world. I think that all of America was pulling for old George. There was a certain spirit about George, something different. He was a changed man. As a young fighter, George Foreman was an angry young man off the streets. He always had a snarl on his face—he wore a mean look and did not talk much to the press. When he came out this time, we saw a smiling, friendly man, quite articulate with a great deal of wisdom. His genuineness and the spirit about him captured all of our imaginations and everybody was pulling for George.

There were some things about George that made him powerful that we can all learn from. He came back with a more relaxed fighting style and more stamina to last through the fights. I was struck by how he never sat down between the rounds. Why not? Powerful people don't sit on their dreams. If you want to be a powerful person, I'm suggesting don't sit on your dreams, don't sit on your ideas. Stand up for what you believe in and go for it, come what may. George refused to sit down. He was saying, "If I sit down, I might not be able to get back up again." It's hard starting all over again. It's very difficult after you sit there for so long, you get comfortable, and dragging yourself back into the race again, to get back into the arena again, to get back in condition again, to get back into the classroom again, to start studying again—it's challenging.

You can do it, but it's very challenging. When George decided not to sit down between the rounds, it's as if he was saying, "That young boy can sit down if he wants to, but I'm sending him a statement by the mere fact that I'm standing up." Everybody was standing with George. As George continued to move forward taking some punishing blows he looked unfazed—there was a look of determination on his face. That's something that powerful people have—determination and purpose.

If you want to be a powerful person, you have got to develop a determined spirit. When life strikes you with some punishing blows—and that's going to happen—when it looks like you just can't make it and you don't have anything left in you, you will get some energy deep down in your guts that you didn't even know you had there. You will be determined to get some power from on high, to believe that life at some point just won't let you get knocked down. That's what powerful people do. They look superhuman because as ordinary people they put themselves into extraordinary situations and they have to perform extraordinarily.

We all have the capacity to do that, but most of us never put ourselves at risk. Most of us never put all of our stuff on the line like these powerful people we admire. No, George did not sit down on his dream.

I'm suggesting that if you want to become a powerful person, you've got to take a stand today. Be honest. Decide that you're not going to take a shortcut. Decide that you are going to draw the line in your life, that there are certain things you just won't tolerate. Decide that you're not going to compromise. There are certain things in your life that are non-negotiable.

When I look at where I want to go and what I want to do, and the impact that I want to make with my life, it's non-negotiable. When it comes to the standard of living that I want to enjoy for myself and for my family—my children are not going to go hungry, my mother will not go hungry—that's non-negotiable. It's not an iffy situation. There is no discussion around this. Well, maybe if this happens, then I'm powerless. No. It's non-negotiable. Find something in your life that is non-negotiable, that you draw the line and say, "I'm not going to do this no matter what."

A friend of mine had an opportunity to go into business and a former classmate of ours offered him some money, saying, "I'll help you out." We both knew he was a drug dealer. As bad as my friend wanted to go into business, he said, "I can't start an honest, clean business with dirty money. Thank you, but no thank you." It would have been an easy shortcut but that was non-negotiable. He had standards and I respect him to this day for his decision. It took him much longer—about three years—to start the business at the level he wanted, but he refused to start instantly because he had standards. He had a sense of integrity with himself and said, "I'm not going to start a business on dirty money."

I respect someone like that. When you just start working on your dream and to develop yourself, life will present some things to you that look easy, that say, "It's just a quick shortcut. Nobody will know." Somebody will know. You will know. You will know within yourself. You will know when you compromise who you are, when you're not honoring yourself, and you erode your self-esteem and your self-appreciation. George Foreman was true to himself. George decided that he was going to pursue his dream. He conditioned himself. He worked hard to develop himself. He gave a respectable showing. He never fell down. He stood up and we all stood with him. He showed himself to be a powerful person. His life changed. I think he activated many people to develop the heart and the courage to go after their dreams. Many people who had written themselves off saying, "I'm too old" or "It's too late." I think many people decided, "Wait a minute. If George can do it, I can do it."

The fact is that when you decide to do it you are going to focus your energy and concentrate. There will be many people, as they told George, "You can't do it, and you're too old." There were likely some moments that he questioned himself, times those knees wanted to buckle, and that his mind said, "George, take a stool and sit-down man. Come on. You're old, nobody's going to laugh. Everybody will understand. You can quit now. You've got the money you need."

I'm sure there were times that he wanted to give up and throw in the towel and say, "Okay. I've made my point." But because he wanted to be true to himself, he didn't do that. There are times that this is going to happen to you, and it's going to happen to me. Whatever powerful people do, they take full responsibility for it. There is a willingness on their part to face the consequences of their actions and a willingness to do whatever is necessary to make things happen. Earl Nightingale said, "We are all self-made, but only the successful will admit it." Powerful people are people who will willingly say, "I made a mistake. I was wrong. I misjudged that and I'm learning from this experience and moving on." They don't try and cover it up. They face the flak, take the criticism, and they move on.

A friend of mine was going into recovery after years of drug and alcohol addiction. He was talking about how challenging it was and that he was dreading going cold turkey. I said, "What do you want me to tell you? That it's going to be a picnic? No, it's not. It's going to kick your butt. Are you going to want to die? Yes, that's a part of it, but that's just what you must go through in order to get where you want to go. Guess what, you are strong enough to do it. You're strong enough and your life is worth whatever you have to go through to get past this addiction, whatever you have to do. This dream you have—will it be easy to just run out and do it? No. Would it happen overnight? No. Would it be a struggle? Yes. Will there be times when you can't make ends meet? Yes, that's a part of it."

Will there be times you won't know what to do? Yes, that's a part of it. Will you have some opposition when things go wrong sometimes? You will have many visits from Murphy. Did somebody ever tell us, somewhere along the way, "Oh, life is going to be really easy?" Probably not. But if they told you that I've got a special announcement, they lied. It can happen. I had a special piece of legislation I wanted to get passed. I said to a fellow representative, "Can I count on your vote?" He said yes. "Look here, if I can't count on it, let me know. There's another rep that owes me chip and I can call on that. I won't need your vote, but I do need you if you say you're going to do it, to do it." He said, "You can count on it." Legislation came up. He voted against my bill, I went back to him and said, "I told you I needed the vote, but if you couldn't give it up, let me know and I will get somebody else. Why didn't you tell me?" He said, "I lied." I was in shock.

How many times has life just worn you out? You didn't expect that. You thought you go to school, get good grades, get a job, living happily ever after and you say, "They lied." Yes, they did. They never told me. You know that song that goes, "Mama told me there'll be days like this." They even tell us that somethings about life are challenging. That's called life. There are challenges like that.

Accept yourself and then accept the fear as a fact and not a force. If you go through life being afraid, people can sense that. They can pick up that fear. That's why you've got to stand up inside yourself. I'm reminded of a little boy that was on a bus and some bigger fellows were picking at him. He wanted to move from them. They were thumping him on the head. He stood up to get away from them and they would push him back down. He would stand up again, they pushed him back down and held him down. He said, "You might hold me down, but I'm standing up inside myself."

That's what we've got to do in life. There will be things that will happen to you in life that will get you down, but you must always stand up inside yourself and know that you can handle this, know that you're capable, because when you develop that kind of spirit, that kind of consciousness, it affects everything around you. You know that there are some people that when they walk, everybody in the neighborhood comes chasing them because they just look like somebody ought to chase them. And then there are those who carry themselves in such a way that nobody wants to mess with them. You want to stand up inside of yourself. When you're facing any kind of challenge, carry yourself in a spirit of strength and knowing and faith, and begin to know that you have what it takes, what is required to create what you want.

Another quality about powerful people is they don't waste any time answering their critics. There has never been a statue erected to a critic. Powerful people listen, they take it into consideration, and they keep on keeping on. Small people try and get even. Many people would rather get even then get ahead. I think that powerful people know that they will always have critics, know there will always be people that will tell you what you cannot do, know there will always be people that will be a thorn in your side working against you, but importantly, know you've got to keep the main focus on your goals and continue to work on your agenda.

Powerful people are people who are focused. They know where they are going. They are lasered in on what it is they have to do. They're learning everything they can about it. They are never satisfied. They are constantly trying to find ways to do it better, to improve on what they're doing. They are not sitting back on their laurels. Powerful people find a way to keep themselves hungry. When you stop being hungry, when you stop finding ways in which you can challenge yourself to do more, when you become satisfied, when you believe that you have hit your peak, when you believe in perfection—which doesn't exist—that's when you begin to lose your grip.

They won't call you "champ" anymore if you go around thinking that you've done all that you can do and that's it. Today, history is not only being read, it's being written. Today, you have to run just to stand still. Things are changing so rapidly. Today, if you want to become a powerful person, you've got to be the kind of person that will never become satisfied with yourself, knowing deep within you that whatever you have done, it's only a tip of the iceberg of what's possible for you.

Challenge yourself to become better. Challenge yourself to work on different areas of yourself to improve. Ask yourself questions constantly. How is it that I can do this better? Get the counsel of people around you. Surround yourself with people who know more than you, people who you can grow from, people who you can learn from, and people who can enrich and enhance your life and enable you to transcend yourself. Powerful people surround themselves with other powerful people. Not yes men or yes women, but people who will challenge them, who will make them stand strong on what they believe and prove it and put their stuff out there before people to examine it.

Powerful people have a sense of mission. I think that when you have a sense of mission—a higher purpose for your life—it gives your life a certain kind of fortification. I'd say you need to fortify yourself. You need to think what is it that I stand for? What three things do I want people to say about me if I die today? What is it that my life represents? What kind of statement am I making with my life? What will be said about you when you leave this industry? What kind of mark are you going to leave on planet Earth? What cause do you believe that you need to be involved in that you can pour yourself into like George did?

It might be in the environment. It might be developing our youth. It might be providing for our senior citizens. What is it? Today powerful people are people who are not intimidated by change, but are driving change. While other people are complaining, saying, "We don't have enough resources to do what we have to do as it is," powerful people take on more responsibility. They do whatever is required to get the job done. They come up with results as opposed to reasons. They deliver.

That's why people love powerful people. As Denis Waitley would say, "They *make* things happen. They don't just *let* things happen." They don't see themselves as victims. They see themselves as being able to have control over their destiny. They are innovators. They are creative. They are making things happen in a new kind of way. There is a famous quotation by Ralph Waldo Emerson, "Do not go where the path may lead, go instead where there's no path and leave a trail." Are you leaving a trail? What kind of legacy are you leaving behind?

Do you see yourself as a powerful person? If not, what is it that you need to do? What is it that you need to change about yourself? What is it that you need to work on to begin to develop yourself into the powerful person that you have within you? Where is it that you have been surrendering and giving up on who you really are? Where is it that you have compromised? Where do you need to draw the line and say, "Here I stand for I can do no other?"

You have it within you to be a powerful person, to take a stand, to operate out of a sense of integrity, to honor yourself as your word, to take on more challenges in life, to begin to embrace the challenges of life as opposed to running from them as many people do. To be willing to face defeat and disappointment and criticism and ridicule again and again and come back, because this gives meaning and value to your life and because you can do no other.

eight

FIND A CAUSE

Everything a man does for himself he takes to his grave with him, but everything he does for others he leaves behind. Start to develop generational thinking. What can I leave for generations yet unborn? Wherever we are, all of us have the capacity to manifest greatness. All of us have the capacity to participate in the game called life and to make a contribution. All of us have a responsibility to give something back because someone paid a price for us to be here. As we begin to look toward the future, we must ask ourselves the question, "What kind of legacy do I want to leave?" There is a professional dimension to our lives, but we also want to look at our social agenda.

What kind of contribution do I want to leave? This can cover a wide variety of interests, issues and causes, from the ecology of the planet to defining some new social order, from assisting senior citizens to decreasing the teenage pregnancy or dropout rates. How can we develop an environment where we value teachers, those who shape the minds of our future and see them in a different kind of role? Or we can contribute to education, to ensure that we are preparing our kids adequately, so they will have all the tools necessary to shape a new destiny for themselves. What can we give back? How is it that we can give something today that will make a difference tomorrow?

I love the work that I do speaking and training for corporations, but I get the greatest joy working with young people. I hope that you find a cause you feel as strongly about as I do about my work with kids. I use various techniques in classrooms and I want to share one of my favorite experiences. In one particular school I asked for the most challenging kids they had. I love to work with kids in special education because I was in that category when I was in high school. When I came in these kids were just tearing up their classroom. They were playing their music, they were fighting and some were playing cards. Generally, they were having a ball.

I stood for a moment looking at them and then went into one of my acts, I started talking to myself. I was mumbling and some of them tried to hear what was going on about, asking, "Who is this guy?" I was talking to myself, saying, "There is greatness in this room. There's greatness. I know it's here." I started looking at the students and caught some of their attention. Now they were saying, "Hey, listen. Listen to this guy." "There's greatness in this room. I know you're here. I can feel your vibration. There's greatness in this room, where are you? There's somebody in this room that I'm in tune with. I know that you're here and you're not supposed to be here. You're just passing through. Who are you?" I walked toward a young man on my right and asked, "Is it you, brother?" He said, "No, no, it's not me." I walked to a young lady and said, "It's you." I was moving quickly and got right in their faces. "Is it you?" "No, no, no, it's not me." "There's somebody here that has greatness in them. I can feel your vibration. Where are you?" I looked around the room real quick and finally, a little fellow in the back, the shortest kid in the room, stood up and said, "Here, I am." I said, "Yes, I knew that you would stand." I said, "But the truth of the matter is, there is greatness in everybody in this room. Over the next two weeks, you are going to discover something about yourself that you don't know."

When I ask the question "There is greatness in this room, where are you?" you will all respond. We began my intensive program, an interactive training process that gave them a larger vision of themselves, that decreased their level of unconscious self-hatred, that gave their lives a sense of purpose, meaning and direction, and taught them systematic thinking for their goals, how to make relationships work, and how to project and see themselves in the future. At the end of that seminar, I asked, "There is greatness in this room, where are you?" All of them stood simultaneously and said, "Here, I am."

I believe that more than anything I do, regardless of the money that I earn, or what I'm able to acquire because of my success, this work has more value and you can't put a dollar figure on that. That gives me more satisfaction and more meaning in my life than anything else I do. I hope that you find something like this in your life. What is it? What cause do you need to be involved in where you can make a difference? Just think about it. What talents do you have right now? What skills? Maybe you're already retired and think you've already done your part. I believe that the fact that you're still breathing means you're not through yet. Your business on earth is not yet completed; you still have something to give. I'm thinking of Mother Teresa, giving her life to the poor in India. I'm thinking of Rosa Parks who started the Rosa and Raymond Parks Institute for youth development and civil rights education and advocacy.

Dr. Johnnie Colemon was an influential minister and teacher who founded the largest church in Chicago seating over 4,000 people. Barack Obama spoke there as both a senator and as President. She founded several other large organizations that serve the community including a large meal service facility that feeds over 600 people after church services, and a school and curriculum to develop the consciousness of young people from around the world. She believed we were entering a new era of consciousness and worked tirelessly into her late 80s to promote her dreams.

I'm reminded of the story of some explorers in Africa who saw some boys playing with these little rocks. They were playing a game similar to shooting marbles, and their marbles were these shiny little rocks. They gave the boys some candy and when they liked it they agreed to trade their marbles for more. Of course they discovered these shiny rocks were actually large uncut diamonds. The young boys had a fortune in their hands, but they didn't know it. Many of us have talents, skills, ability, the consciousness to make tremendous difference in life and we don't know it.

If I had operated out of a limited vision of myself, I would be working in some type of mediocre capacity. If I had bought into my environment, if I had believed the things that the educational system had said to me or what my friends had said to me, if I'd been concerned about failing or facing rejection or defeat or not making it or being dumb or not making any mistakes, I would still be in Overtown or Liberty City. But because of someone believing in me at a time when I did not believe in myself, and seeing something in me when I did not, I was able to develop a vision of myself in the future and realize, "There's got to be more."

As a child I used to travel with my mother back to our home in Overtown after she finished working in Miami Beach. I used to wonder why we couldn't stay. All the wealth and opulence there and fabulous hotels like the Fontainebleau Hotel. "Why can't we live there too, mama? Why can't we have that big house over there?" I just could not understand why. Why couldn't we enjoy that standard of living? Many people accepted that as their destiny, but there was something in me that said no. I used to just daydream as a kid, living where I wanted to live, doing what I wanted to do. I daydreamed and had a vision of a better life. Try doing that now. I want you to see yourself doing more. What is it that you'd like to do right now? If you were to die today, what are three things that you helped to create and make it a better world?

I wanted to improve my environment. I wanted to improve my circumstances. I had a vision of myself being able to earn enough money to make a difference in the lives of kids, as someone had made a difference in my life. Just as Mr. Washington had when he looked at me and said, "Young man, you've got greatness within you." I wanted to do that. That's been my dream. I live with that. I have this vision of being able to touch the lives of young kids, to touch the lives of people around the planet. That's my personal crusade and mission. I don't want to be a hero. You don't do it because you want a banquet or a plaque or to see your name in the newspapers. You do it because it's who you are, because all of us are who we are, because somebody has made a sacrifice. Somebody has made a contribution. Somebody has given us a hand up. Somebody was there for us when we needed it. None of us make it by ourselves.

What is a cause that you can become involved in? I tell you that it can give a lot of power to your life, a lot of meaning. My friend, a retired cook, works at a church in Detroit. You can tell he loves it when he serves you, the way he dips up the food. When you receive the plate, you know whoever assembled this food on this plate loves what they do. I have another friend who provides a level of love and care and nurturing for people facing terminal illness and their families. She says, "I just love to work with people. I love giving back. I love sharing." Another friend helps senior citizens to develop physical exercise routines and to practice yoga, so they can have more physical movement and are able to get around and live independently. What is it that you can become involved in? How can you give something back? I believe that when you have faced some real difficulties and challenges in life, that's when you can really appreciate giving back. That's when you can really appreciate sharing who you are because it gives your life a special kind of power. I think that the people who make the greatest difference in life are the people who are the givers.

I've seen people who couldn't afford to give financially and gave what they could, people who are physically challenged or facing death themselves, becoming a comfort to other people. I recall a young girl at the Ronald McDonald House, where families with sick children can stay and get care. Genève was staying there, suffering from cancer and terminally ill herself. Another patient resident had completely withdrawn and wouldn't talk, even to his family. Genève huddled with him in a corner and afterward, he began to open up and was very positive, receptive and loving to his family and others. She told me that she said to him over and over, "You're going to be all right." She was a comfort to him, a positive little energy. She visited all the rooms, cheering up all as she went. Little Genève, only eleven, who had her own cross to bear, found a way to give something back, to share her greatness. I say there's a Genève in you. Regardless of where your life is, all of us showed up to give something back. As you lose yourself in giving, you literally gain your life. As you pour yourself into the universe, into your work, and making a difference where you are with what you showed up with, you'll gain a life that you can be proud of.

I was called upon to speak to a group of kids in Los Angeles—during a time when the death rate of kids being victims of drive-by shootings had skyrocketed. I wanted to go to Los Angeles and make a difference, to make an impact. I was told there would be over 700 people there for me speak with. I changed my schedule and went there at my own expense. When I arrived, there were only a handful of kids, not more than seven or eight. I was angry. I felt it was a waste of my time. I had an attitude. I did not give my best. After I spoke, I let it be known that I did not appreciate that 700 attendees has been promised but so few had shown up. They took me back to the hotel.

Around 3:00 that morning, I got a call from the minister who had sponsored the workshop who said, "I'm sorry to call you this time of morning, but Kenyatta, one of the young men who was at the talk tonight, wants to talk to you. His twin brother was one of the kids killed in a drive-by shooting. He'd like to talk to you. I've asked him not to call you but he insisted. Would you please talk to him for a moment?"

"What?" I said, "Okay, put him on the phone." I'm irritated now. Kenyatta said, "Mr. Brown, when you came to speak, you did not give your best and I was really disappointed with you. I've listened to your tapes and you said you must deal with circumstances such as they are. Regardless of what, do your best, regardless." I said, "Wait a minute. They promised me at least 700 kids would be there. My time is very valuable. I drove a long distance to be there. The least they could have done is put people in the room. I don't have time to waste with organizations that can't keep their commitments."

This young boy said, "I listened to your tapes for a long time. I've grown to admire you. Among the things I heard you say on your tapes was you must deal with circumstances such as you find them. You came in this evening and I admit, we did not have the numbers that you asked for. We did not deliver as we had promised we would, but we were looking for you, the motivator, to give us some hope. We are depressed and we don't know what to do. We were looking for some direction and you were so caught up and pouting with your ego because we didn't have the place full. You didn't give us your best."

I rolled out of bed and I gave this young boy my best argument. He would not relent. He would not give up. Finally, I said, "Okay. I apologize." He said, "Good. It takes a big man to do that." I learned something important from that experience—that we can always give some kind of excuse or justification for not giving our best. It really didn't matter that 700 people weren't there. If just six or three show up, that's all I'm responsible for, and I should give them my very best, regardless.

The press wasn't there. The cameras weren't there. The television stations weren't there, that's not important. My job is to give my best, period. That's what I showed up to do. I learned a great deal from that. That was a lesson for me. Whenever I speak, I don't care if it's only one person in the room. When I leave there, I would leave there drenching wet from perspiration because I'm going to work to give my best regardless of the circumstances. When we look at the conditions that exist in society, right now more than ever, we need people, we need men and women to step forward, to take a stand, to make a difference.

Ask yourself, "What do I stand for? What kind of stand can I take with my life right now that will make a tremendous difference?" I believe that the reason most people go through life being spectators, go through life being takers rather than givers is because they have a limited vision of themselves. They can't see themselves making a difference. It doesn't matter how huge the problem is. It doesn't matter how disastrous things appear to be. Human beings have the capacity to take the most disastrous circumstances and make something positive and powerful and meaningful out of it.

Look at your life right now and ask yourself, "How is it that I can give something back?"

What do I stand for? What is the philosophy of my life? What do I truly believe in? What stand, what cause, what belief, am I willing to give up my life for? Chaplain Peter Marshall said, "Unless we stand for something, we shall fall for anything." Where will you draw the line and say, "I won't cross this line? I will not compromise." In his book, *Critique of Pure Reasoning*, Immanuel Kant said, "Sometimes, we must give out of a sense of oughtness, that certain things happen that we just say something ought to be done about this." As Socrates said, "The uncommitted life isn't worth living." What are you willing to commit your life to, so that your living would not have been in vain? There is a saying, "Life is God's gift to us. The way we live it is our gift to god."

nine

THE COURAGE TO CONFRONT YOUR FEARS

How do we find the courage to do the things we know we must do? How can we face our challenges, deal with setbacks and take on new opportunities? How do we develop an attitude of "I can do it?" When you are faced with any new dilemma or situation, you have to go right into the center of it. Look at the situation, examine it very closely, and then you can decide to take it on. If you try to go around it, if you try to compromise, if you try to negotiate it, it won't work. You got to face it head on. It's normal that you're going to feel some fear. There's a book by Susan Jeffers, *Feel the Fear and Do It Anyway,* a classic self-help book that outlines what we fear, why we feel it and what to do about it. The title alone gives us a roadmap—first, feel that fear, and then you can confront it and go on anyway.

That happens in a lot of situations. I had to discipline my second oldest son. As a parent you have to get comfortable doing this. At some point in time, because of their inexperience and lack of wisdom, you're going to need to do this. There are clear disciplines you will need to enforce, certain restrictions they must learn to live with, and decisions that you'll have to make. The kids don't have enough maturity to appreciate what and why you're doing these things. They may understand when they're older but now they're going to hate you for it. You must have the courage to do what is right in spite of that.

In this particular situation, my son was a student at Ohio State University, and doing poorly. I said, "I'm not going to subsidize Ds and Fs. You either bring your grades up to a minimum of a B or I can't give you any more financial support." He was very upset about that but I really did not care how upset he was anymore because I'd gotten to my wit's end. I believed I had done everything I could, but I realized I had not dealt with the situation effectively. I finally said, "Hey, wait a minute. I'm not dealing with him like a man." He can't grow from this kind of wimpy parenting that I'm providing.

I took a stand. I said, "I'm not going to support you anymore." The next semester he worked hard and got all As and Bs. If I had not taken that stand, if I had continued to subsidize his Ds, Fs and even Cs, he still would be doing that. What if he had dropped out of school because of the lack of financial support? So be it. He's a grown man. He's got to learn to fly under the strength of his own wings.

I had another situation with someone very close to me. We had a relationship where we were each pretending not to know what we both knew. I pretended not to know that he was an alcoholic, and he pretended not to know that I knew. The discussion never came up until I finally had to deal with it. Another mutual friend said, "If you really love and care about him, why don't you face it with him so that he can get some help?" I asked myself what I was afraid would happen. I visualized the worst thing that could happen when I said, "Hey, you've got a problem." He could deny it and say, "I take exception to that." He could get upset with me. He could get angry. He could say, "Go to hell. Don't talk to me anymore." It could destroy our friendship. Could I live with that? I had to deal with that.

Finally, after visualizing it over and over again, with each worst-case scenario I learned to see myself as being able to handle it. Each time I played that tape back in my mind, I saw myself telling him. I saw him going off the deep end and each time I saw myself being able to handle it. Finally, I was able to confront him. I said, "I'd like to help you. You've got a drinking problem and I'd like to be a support to you." He denied it.

I was strong. This is a man that I love and admire very much who's had tremendous impact in my life. I had to take him on. I stepped closer and said, "Yes, you do have a problem. I want to help you get some help." Eventually after a long conversation he agreed to get help. When we said goodbye and I went home, I was completely exhausted. I was drained. But I had done it. I agonized over it for a long time and it took everything in me. But I found out I could do it and it was not as bad as I had imagined.

I used to have a tremendous inferiority complex about speaking before people that I felt had more going for them than I did. I'm not college trained and I felt that college educated people were the most intelligent people on the planet, that I had nothing to say to them. Why would they listen to me? That's the way I felt. I had to visualize myself speaking before various audiences that I thought had more going for them. I had to realize my own value and appreciate that I was a worthwhile person, even though I didn't have the background, money, or education that they had.

Part of the process is seeing yourself being worthy, being capable, and having what you need. Understand that you're more than able; you deserve to be listened to or to have that dream and that passion. Whatever it is that you envision for yourself, you've got to see in your mind's eye and know that you've got what it takes. Here is an affirmation to read and recite out loud:

I see in my mind's eye.
I see myself confronting my fears.
I see myself feeling my fears.
I see myself handling my fears.
I'm more than able.
I've got the right stuff.

It's good to know you have the right stuff. In *The Magic of Thinking Big*, David J. Schwartz says, "Action cures fear." When you take some action, when you imagine the worst possible scenario and then move on and do something, you can lose that fear. Instead of being immobilized by fear, you are energized by it. If you accept yourself and you see yourself beyond your fears, then you don't accept yourself as a victim. You begin to see that you are more important than any fear that you have. You are more powerful than any fear that you have.

People make their fear more powerful than they are. They make their fear more powerful than their dreams. Let's make every one of us and what we want more powerful than fear. Eleanor Roosevelt said, "I believe that anyone can conquer fear by first doing three things. Do it once to demonstrate, to prove to yourself that you can do it. Do it the second time to see whether or not you like it. Then, do it again to see that you want to keep on doing."

By tapping into third step, you're already through that fear and you've handled it most effectively. Begin to know and accept yourself as the person to do what it is that you want to do and that you have the courage to get beyond whatever is holding you back, whether it's fear, procrastination, insecurity. You're not going to allow that to stop you. You're going to get past that. You're going to move on, to confront and to conquer whatever is holding you back. We will not hide out behind our fears.

If you don't see yourself as deserving what you want, you can hide out behind that fear; use all kinds of excuses that keep you from venturing out into the real arena of life. Jack Reid said, "When you realize that we are utilizing only a very small percentage of our potential, that thought itself can drive us past any fear, so decide it. You look at your life as you look into the future and say, 'What fears am I holding on to? What fears that I'm allowing to imprison me, that are keeping me from breaking out, keeping me from living up to my true potential, keeping me from really being happy, keeping me from having a sense of adventure and excitement in my life? What's keeping me from controlling my destiny?'"

When you accept yourself and you accept fear as a fact, that means that fear is another something that happens, another something that you're going to experience. But it is not a force to hold you back. It doesn't have any special power other than what you give it. You accept the fact that you are afraid and then you move on anyhow. You move on, you go past it, and you do whatever you've got to do.

I had a situation where I had to speak at a big rally. It was in a stadium, with 17,000 people and I was nervous. My inner conversation was there's absolutely no way that I can connect with this audience. There will be so many lights in my eyes, and I'll go out there, my thoughts will not be flowing, they're going to boo me off the stage, people are going to be talking and making all kinds of noise. I was programming myself to go out there and flop. As I continued to think about it, and I made the mistake of peeping out at the audience, I became even more panic-stricken. I said to the guy, "I just can't go out there." He said, "What do you mean? Are you crazy?" I said, "I don't know what's happening right now." I'm suffering from shortness of breath and things were happening to me physically. I knew that I was unconsciously sabotaging this moment that I had been working for, that I was becoming gripped in fear. Something said, "You have got to handle this." Finally, I kept saying, "Les, you can do it, you can do it, you can do it." I started breathing deeply. I remembered the technique my friend Pat taught me, "When you're faced with a frightening situation, take a deep breath and see yourself taking in strength which makes you more than able and capable of handling it." I did that. I took in a deep breath and I said to myself, "I own this audience." I went out there and I wore them out.

Take a deep breath and see yourself being more than capable of doing it, of taking it on and handling it. Another technique is to see yourself beyond that particular situation, with it already resolved. Some people call it the "as-if" formula. See yourself resolving the situation, handling it, see it already taken care of and everything worked out fine. No problems. It just happened the way you wanted it to happen.

A friend who was in Vietnam says anytime he's confronted with a major situation, he remembers when he was in Vietnam and says, "Hey, if I could handle that, I can handle this." Can you find some kind of experience in your life that took great courage on your part to deal with? Now look back and relive that experience in your mind. Remember what it took, whatever you had to dig up from deep within yourself to enable you to act, and then you call on that. Remember that moment when you were able to move forward, to handle the situation. Remember that you did that once. The Vietnam vet says it perfectly, "If I could handle that, surely this is nothing but whipped cream."

Many people are motivated by negative consequences. Look at the situation and ask yourself, what's the negative impact of my not handling this? If I continue to put this off, what will happen then? Think about that. If you don't handle it, and you keep on, pretending not to know what you know, it won't go away or disappear by magic and you will find yourself in a very perilous situation.

Looking at the negative consequences might motivate you to handle it. Another exercise to help you to call on the courage within yourself is to write down three strong reasons why you must take action. Or perhaps you have got to take action because this has gone too far and you just have no choice. The first time I had to fire someone, I did not want to do it. I decided to hide behind my business manager and was going to just have him handle the termination when I was away, so I wouldn't be involved. Don't tell me about it, just fire him. Just later on, about a month later on, I realized they're gone all right. I want to be the good guy. I mean, I'm a wimp, a coward. Then I said, "Wait a minute, I can't do this. I have to handle this myself. I can't live with myself, if I do it like this, if I take the coward's way out." This was not the way to handle it.

I wrote down three reasons why I had to fire my employee. As I read those reasons, I realized, "I have no reason to be a wimp about this. I had been more than fair." So I called the person in and said, "I've known you for a long time. We've been together for many years and you know I care about you. I appreciate everything you've done for me and what you've contributed to my business. Here's what we both know. This relationship is not working now. We don't have to stop being friends, but you can no longer work here. I will help you in any way to find another position but I'm telling you that I must let you go."

I replayed that in my mind over and over again. I've known this person since high school and we're like relatives. We've been through all kinds of things together. Here I was with a very close friend that I had to tell, "You're fired." It was rough. Yet I did it and felt so much better within myself. It was not as bad as I had imagined it. When you continuously avoid making courageous decisions, you erode your self-esteem. You don't feel good about yourself. You feel like a wimp. When you know you need to do something and you don't do it, when you don't take care of business, it eats at you. We can make ourselves sick, not taking care of things we know we should take care of.

How do you keep on keeping on and not lose your drive, not lose enthusiasm, not be discouraged? Much has to do with how you learn to process things within yourself. You begin to know that if you don't get the results you want, that it doesn't make you any less of a person. This is what you have to walk through. These are the doors you have to go through. These are the hoops that you've got to flip through. Part of being successful is that you've got to learn to live with failures and defeats and disappointments. It goes with the territory. You cannot reach your goal, you cannot achieve the greatness that you want to achieve, and you cannot experience the rewards of success without going through this. We're just being realistic about it since it goes with the territory. You decide to handle it, to suck up the wind within yourself and to go forward. You learn it's not going to kill you. Learn what you must learn from it, handle it and keep on keeping on until you reach your destination.

Let's take a moment to name some of our overwhelming fears that can have devastating effects on our dreams and aspirations. They include the fear of not being liked, the fear of not making it, and the fear of success, which is really the fear of failure. The fear of success was a big monster I had to face. I thought that if I made it, I couldn't handle it and eventually I'd be exposed for the incompetent, inferior person that I am and I would blow it all. The fear of success is really the fear of failure of not being able to hold on, of not being able to make it happen to stay in the game.

When we have those kinds of fears, they become self-fulfilling prophecies because we focus on them and they become our predominant state of mind. What do you do about that? I think it's important for us to once again review why you are in the game. What are your reasons for being out here? What is it that you can think about that can give you a sense of strength and courage and faith to step into the fear and do what you must do anyhow? How do you do that? Some people have to get angry. The fear of poverty is one that I have where I've resolved I'm not going to ever be poor. I didn't like what that life was like for me and feared the many limitations that come with poverty—not being in charge of my destiny, not being able to determine my own worth, not being able to determine how much I can earn, not being able to provide the quality of life and proper health care for myself or my family. I cannot see giving up that kind of control in my life. That kind of fear drives me. Fear can immobilize you or fear can propel you. It can motivate you. It can inspire you. You've got to decide to let fear work for you. You see, I'm actually afraid not to pursue my dream.

I'm especially afraid not to go after what I feel I can do because I fear that day when I'm old, having regrets, "Oh, if I only had my life to live over again." At one seminar I asked "Does anybody has anything brave to say?" An eighty-seven-year-old woman stood up and said, "If I had my life to live over again, I would have taken more chances. All my life I've sacrificed myself and my dreams in deference to my husband and children. I never did anything for me. All my life I pleased everybody but myself. I never took any chances. I was always playing it safe."

She went on, "I don't have my life to live over and with the time that I have left, I'm going to take more chances. I'm going to do what I want to do." All of us in the room that day resolved, "This thing called fear is only what we choose to make it. Is it really such a biggie? No, it is not." We can decide, "I'm afraid not to take care of business. I'm afraid not to take a chance on myself."

What's the worst thing that can happen? Everybody might hate me? I lose all my money? What's the worst thing that can happen if I decide to take a chance on me? People laugh at me? That's a possibility. I could become broke, so? I can come back again. My wealth is not determined based upon what I have. My wealth is determined by who I am. The reason nobody will shed a tear if a rich man like Ted Turner or Jeff Bezos lost every dime is because we know these men have the capacity to do it again. You're not determined by what you have. You're determined by who you are.

Part of overcoming fear is to develop an ongoing strategy, a plan of action of self-empowerment. Take time to listen to tapes, take time to go to seminars, take time to read books that inspire you. As you read inspirational stories about other individuals like I do, say, "If this guy can do it or if she can do it, I can do it." Surround yourself with people who are doing what you want to do. As you look at them, you'll see yourself doing it and monitor yourself—realizing that you are more than able. You were born for this, you have the power within you to live your dream.

As you read and feed your mind with the pictures and the dreams and the words that empower you, you become inspired. As you continuously surround yourself with people who are also growing, developing, expanding themselves and their horizons, who have zeal and a sense of adventure, you become motivated. Being around that kind of environment stimulates you. You're encouraged to think, "Hey, I can do it too." You find yourself doing little things to develop. Then you start growing and gaining confidence. Eventually, the fear that you experience will be something you can use as a tool to your advantage.

Every time I speak, I'm afraid. I'm always nervous. I use that fear to go up and take care of business. I don't take anything for granted. You can dispel fear by being competent. Let that drive you to do your homework, to work hard at developing technical mastery, so that whatever comes, you will handle it because you *can* handle it.

Here are some affirmations that I want you to write down and repeat daily.

I know what I want in life and I have the courage to do whatever it takes to get it.

I have the power to handle whatever comes up.

This is my decade. (Every year, I used to say this is my year, but one good year won't be enough for me. I believe that if the universe will give us a year, they'll give us a decade. Why limit ourselves? Just get that attitude.)

I know I can move confidently through all of the challenges that confront me.

I am worthwhile, talented, and deserve to achieve my goals.

We're going to end with some consideration of that word "*deserve.*" This is a key concept. When we start to investigate why people fail to achieve their greatness, never go after their goals, or why they procrastinate and don't prepare or develop themselves we discover the primary reason is because they don't feel worthy. When you feel worthy, there are certain things that you just won't tolerate. You simply just won't put up with them.

Only when people start to feel worthy can they leave an environment that is not contributing to their growth and development. People who feel worthy can say, "Wait a minute, I can do better than this. This is not who I am." I think this is when a person can put down a glass and say, "I might have been drinking all of these years and throwing my life away, but that's not who I really am. I've been misrepresenting myself. I deserve better than this from me." This is when a procrastinator can say, "I deserve better than this from life. I know what I need to do and I can get started."

Look at your life right now and be honest. Ask yourself where in your life are you not being who you really are? Where do you know you need to take some constructive action? Where can you say, "I deserve better than that, I am better than that?"

A better life begins with a better you and that will happen when you make the decision, "I deserve it."

t e n

GETTING UNSTUCK– OVERCOMING PROBLEMS

How often is it that so many of us get stuck and how often is that we're doing it to ourselves? We consider the things we know that we deserve or want out of life or what we'd like to enjoy and experience, and then we just go sideways and start blocking ourselves. Let's start this chapter with the following affirmation. Write it down and say it out loud daily:

Whatever you're looking at
It belongs to you.
Whatever you're seeking
It's seeking you.
You can have it.

I was reminded of this affirmation after taking a ride with a friend who has been working for a long time in a job where she's been miserable. I said, "If it's that stressful and causing you that much pain, why don't you just find another job, or even be bold and quit and do something else?" I was dismayed to hear her response—which put her in that familiar chorus line with a lot of other people—"I would but . . ." She built a case on why she couldn't do it. That got me thinking about taking a poll and I started talking to other people about their work lives. I'd ask about what they were doing and if it was their passion. Then they would tell me what their real passion was. When I asked, "Why aren't you doing what you really want to do," I heard the same answer over and over, "I can do it, but . . ." Then they would stop. This word, "but," just kept on coming up, along with wouldn't, couldn't, or shouldn't. Occasionally I'd hear, "One day, I'm going to have my own business." All people talk about "one day I'm going to." Some of you know them and some of you get up in the morning and look in the mirror at that person.

I started thinking about all of this and how is it that many times we block ourselves. We use these words, almost like we're in a trance, sleepwalking through life. I think "but" is a dream killer. There a lot of things we want to do, places we'd like to go and things we'd like to experience and we just stop at "but" and we build a case. "But" is an argument for our limitations. When we argue for our limitations, we get to keep them. The limitations I'm talking about here are the excuses that we use to hold ourselves back. It's easy to use these excuses to validate your inaction, continue to procrastinate, and hide out behind fear and not act on your dreams.

Right now more than ever, people need to look for ways to live their dream and to make it on their own. There is no such thing as job security. There's no such thing as a storm-proof life. There are no guarantees today, the illusion is gone. There was a time when we were told if we graduated from high school, went to college, and worked for a company, in thirty years or so we'd get a lovely watch and a golden retirement. If that day ever really existed, it is now gone forever, never to return.

Instead of living in fear, feeling stressed out and powerless, and behaving like victims, I think we can create ways to become an active force in our own lives. Look at ways to take charge of our own destiny. Look at ways to design a life of substance, to truly live our dreams, to get fired up about our lives and really pour ourselves into what we are doing. I think these are some great times to be alive, that there's a new wave of consciousness sweeping the country, that's sweeping the world. We can decide to get on with our lives.

One of the first steps to getting unstuck in life is having a larger vision of yourself. Try seeing yourself in the future—doing and being what it is you want to be. As you hold this vision over a period of time, you will begin to develop the attitude. You begin to develop the consciousness and holding this vision tenaciously will drive you into action to act on what you see. Because your thoughts have magnetic power, you'll begin to attract the circumstances, you attract the people and all of the things you need as you continue to hold this vision. That's why people without vision will perish. People who decide to commit suicide are people who have a limited vision of themselves. They felt like they had no other option. They couldn't see themselves doing better. They couldn't see life being worth it.

Part of what I discovered in my work with the Cook County Jail is that these young men and women do not have a vision of themselves in the future. They don't feel their lives have any value. When you have a way you can see yourself in the future, your vision of yourself will pull you into the future. If you can't see yourself here, then you are subject to do anything. If you don't value yourself—your life has no value and no one else's life around you has any value.

It's easy for people who give up on themselves to give up on life and start abusing themselves with drugs or alcohol. These people do not have a vision of themselves in the future that will help to cultivate and create an attitude that they can make it in spite of the circumstances and challenges of life. Someone asked a jarring question, "Why is it that most people prefer known hells to unknown heavens?" They can't see themselves doing any better. They can't see themselves beyond that particular situation.

I'm reminded of a story of a soldier who was captured in enemy territory. The captain said to him, "You have one of two choices. Tomorrow morning at 5:00, you can face the firing squad or you can go through this door here and beyond this door, unknown horrors. Which do you choose?" A secretary who had observed that meeting came to work early the next morning and heard the firing squad shots ring out and asked the captain, "What's beyond that door?" He said, "Freedom, but very few people will choose it." People have a fear of the unknown. They don't know what's there. People say, "What will the future bring?" The future will bring whatever you show up with.

Are you working on yourself now? Are you developing yourself right now? Are you preparing yourself for the future? The Optimist Club says, "The future belongs to those who prepare for it," so don't worry about the future. If you take care of business right now, if you develop yourself right now, you cannot stay stuck, you will outgrow it. If you continue to work to develop yourself, you're seeking growth experiences, you're venturing out, you're learning all you can, you're surrounding yourself with people who are doing more that you can learn and grow from, you'll begin to develop the consciousness to attract everything to you. All of us have areas in our lives where we have to grow. All of us have areas in our lives where we momentarily are stuck and we need some help and assistance. It is always been very easy for me to help people, to give assistance. But one of the most challenging experiences I've ever had was to swallow my ego and pride and to say, "I don't know. Would you help me, please?"

One of the most difficult things is to accept help. To admit that I didn't know or that I was frightened or that I needed some help is so challenging. Ego, many times, won't allow you to do that, won't allow you to admit that you don't know. Part of what can enable us to get unstuck is asking for help. You've got to reach out. You have to keep on working to develop yourself and make a conscious, deliberate, determined effort to have a winning spirit. Regardless of whatever is going on—if you don't have a dime in your pocket, your bills aren't paid, you've just lost a major business, you have to separate who you are from what has happened with your business. You're not a failure.

I've seen people lose their businesses and start all over again, certain and assured. And another who lost his business took it personally. He gave up. He saw himself as a failure and didn't try anything else. I want you to know that's not the way it is. Don't internalize the results you produce if they're not what you want them to be. Do take full responsibility for them and ask what you learned from the experience and how you can grow from that knowledge. And come back again. Let's think about how sports can provide metaphors we can use in life. The team goes out, calls a play, throws a pass, and the receiver drops the pass or there's an interception by the opposition. Do they then say, "Well, we tried to pass, it didn't work. Everybody go home?" No, they go back to the huddle. They come up with another play and they come back to the game. It's the same in business and in life. We come out with a game plan. We check out the opposition, ask what the challenges are we have to overcome, and we implement a play. You don't just give up if it doesn't work, and become frustrated, discouraged and go back home. Rather, you go back to the drawing board. Slumps can happen to many great athletes—baseball player who suddenly can't hit a ball or basketball players missing all their shots. They don't decide, "That's it. I'm not going to play anymore. I'm retiring." To get out of that slump, they have to work their way out. They have to swing their way out. They have to shoot their way out.

The same thing goes for us. We can all have times of getting into a slump. Why? It's called life. Sometimes things are going really well. You can make sales at the snap of your finger. Then sometimes you can't. Sometimes business is going to be real good, people are going to be reliable and everything's going to work out just the way you want. And sometimes, things are just going to be off. You're going to miss planes. People will miss promised delivery times. Bills will not be paid. People you've done work for won't pay you on time. Why? It's called life.

Perhaps it's so we could learn all of these things and grow. We learn how to deal with it. It's called being a human being. What can we learn from this? Sometimes things work out well, sometimes they don't. Do you take it personally? No. I'm reminded of the tale of a man out for a walk, who saw a dog on a porch moaning and groaning. He asked the owner, "Why is this dog moaning and groaning?" The owner replied, "He's lying on a nail." "Why won't he just get up off the nail?" "Oh, it's not hurting badly enough for him to get up, he's just hurting bad enough to moan and groan."

Many people go through life being far more miserable than they have to be. I think of it as the moaning and groaning attitude. We've all encountered this familiar mindset, critical of everything and everyone, complaining about circumstances personal and public. Not realizing they can do something about it. We all showed up with the power, the capacity, and the ability to make a difference on the planet. I think that we often receive detrimental messaging through societal conditioning and the educational process. We learn, "Don't rock the boat," and "Get in line," or "Don't shake things up," and "Don't disturb the status quo." That kind of conditioning can create a kind of victim mentality that many of us operate within.

They are volunteer victims. They volunteer, sign up and sentence themselves to lives of misery, of feeling powerless. They've accepted evading their own true greatness and are not surrounding themselves with people that can nourish, empower, and enable them to transcend themselves. I ran across a study of 3,000 top achievers around the world and discovered that most were not rocket scientists. Most were not the top A students in their schools or colleges; 85% of them had achieved their goals because of their attitude, and 15% because of their aptitude.

I think that attitude is far more important than anything else—more than talent, and more than ability. Your vision of yourself, your attitude about yourself, is something that affects your life and all the people you encounter. We've known students who were brilliant, but because of their attitudes about themselves, other people, and life, they end up being miserable. How many of you work with people like that? You hate to see them come to work because their attitude affects everybody. No one wants to deal with people like that. You just want to keep away from them. I say don't try to change them, because it's a full-time job changing yourself. Look at your attitude right now. Is it what it could be? Do you have a defeated attitude about life? Or do you have a chip on your shoulder that life owes you something? Do you have a story to tell? Has life done you wrong and you've been hurt. Guess what? Everybody has a story. Many have something that's caused unjustifiable pain. If you live long enough, you will experience more of it. Handle it.

I get a lot of inspiration from W. Mitchel and even the title of his book says it all, *It's Not What Happens To You, It's What You Do About It*. Here is a man who overcame two life threatening and life challenging accidents that left him a paraplegic, severely disfigured from burns, and missing most of his fingers. Yet he carries his message forward in books and speaks to us about courage, the human spirit and it's yearning for survival. His story is the answer to our question, "what are you going to do about it?" Ultimately that's the only thing that matters. How long are you going to be stuck before you get on with your life? Decide that you're going to act. Surround yourself with quality people who can remind you of what the possibilities are for your life. I love that saying, "If you want to soar like an eagle, leave those pigeons alone." Decide that you want to soar like an eagle. You're a different kind of breed.

Learn all you can in life and be willing to experiment. I like to say you've got to learn to dance with life. If you don't learn to dance with life, life will pass you by and get another partner. Even if you don't want to, you're going to have to dance with life, so you might as well learn some steps. Life is going to drag you out on the floor anyway, so get out there and try to do the twist.

If you go through life holding back, and most of us do, we run the risk of taking most of our stuff with us to the grave. If we ask ourselves, have we done all we can do, most of us will have to answer, no, we haven't. We've been holding back. We have ideas we don't act on, things we want to do. We are afraid to take chances. We go through life trying to seek security and not coming outside of our comfort zone. The fact that you're still here, still breathing, and reading this book shows you've got some more work to do and you owe it to yourself. When you get up in the morning, you can look yourself in the face and say, "I'm living my life on my terms."

Choose to be an uncommon person. I like this excerpt from *Common Sense*, written in 1776 by Thomas Paine: "I choose not to be a common man. It is my right to be uncommon if I can. I seek opportunity, not security. I do not wish to be a kept citizen, humbled and dulled by having the state look after me. I want to take the calculated risk, to dream and to build, to fail and to succeed. I refuse to live from hand to mouth. I prefer the challenges of life to the guaranteed existence; the thrill of fulfillment to the stale calm of Utopia . . . I will never cower before any master nor bend to any threat. It's my heritage to stand erect, proud and unafraid, to think and act for myself . . . and to face the world boldly and say: This, I have done."

Choose to be uncommon. It's easy to be negative. It's easy to say that it won't happen or it won't work out. It's easy to be down on yourself. It's easy to point out the problems rather than the solutions. However you can choose to be uncommon, to create some new standards and go to another level, to change it and do it, like it has never been done before. If you choose to write some new pages in history, that's a whole different kind of program. And because you aren't a common person, because you do have something special within you, because you do have genius within you, it is your right and your responsibility to bring it on out here.

eleven

YOU GOTTA BE HUNGRY

When I think about a role model for my life, who has had the greatest impact on me, the immediate answer is Mamie Brown. What I realized about my mother is that when she adopted us, she had absolutely no idea how she was going to raise two children by herself. She did day work and adopted twin boys, my brother and me. She had no idea, but five years later she adopted my sister. This is very powerful for me, because I think that many times we don't go for the things we want to do because we look at where we are, and where we want to go, and ask, "How am I going to do it?" and don't get any answers back.

As the familiar Bible quote says, "we walk by faith, not by sight." I believe that life does not give you any answers until you first take the plunge, but you've got to get out there. You've got to be willing to take a chance. You've got to be willing to take a risk and most people go through life playing it safe. If you're not willing to risk, you cannot grow. If you cannot grow, you cannot become your best. If you cannot become your best, you cannot be happy. If you can't be happy, then what else is there? My mother was willing to take a chance. If you had asked her for her plan of action: "How're you going to raise these boys? You've never had any children before. How's it going to work?" there would have been nothing, no plan or track record to point to. That really hit me, that my mother never had any children herself and here she is saying, "I'll take them." Boy, what confidence.

My mother knew within herself that she could do it. Whatever goal you have, you've got to know within yourself that you can do it. My mother operated with an "I can do it" attitude. She couldn't prove it but she knew it. There are certain things you just know. The next thing is that she made the commitment. People who have ever done anything in life made the commitment, they said, "I'm going to do it" They became "no matter what" people just like my mother did. She was determined to provide for us no matter what. Was it hard? Yes. It was very difficult. There were times when we did not have enough food to eat. There was a time my mother was home ill and incapacitated for a long period of time. We had some food in the refrigerator that was suspicious and I asked her if we could eat it. She was worried we might get ill and ate some of it first, saying if she got sick to go get help and if not we could eat it then. I was pacing back and forth with worry and fear, guarding her, asking if she was all right. I think I've always been an old person. She was already perspiring and moaning from the pain of the sickness but finally said, "I'm alright son. It's okay. You can eat the food." Shortly thereafter I answered the door to a minister from a nearby church. I'll never forget that tall man appearing at our door. Reverend Graham said, "I heard there's a family here that needs some food," delivering a food basket at our time of great need. Looking at him I said, "I'd like to be like him." That was the first time I saw my destiny. I would go to church, sit in the back and watch him as he delivered his moving sermons, a master orator. I think at different times we are confronted with our destiny and he was my first brush with great orators and inspirational mentors. Then I saw Mr. Leroy Washington, the Speech and Drama teacher at Booker T. Washington High School, and then again, when I saw Zig Ziglar, and Dr. Norman Vincent Peale, and other great speakers, I said within myself, "I'd like to be like them." After I said, "I like to be like them," there's another part of me, that lower consciousness that said, "But you can't. Who are you? You are nobody. You have no college education, you're 'educable mentally retarded,' you make Fs all the time, you failed twice in school, you're slower than most people. You can't do that, Les Brown, who you fooling? Come on, be realistic."

If you want to do more in life, if you want to reach your goals, I don't think that you can be realistic. I think that you have to be unreasonable if you want to produce unreasonable results in your life. Logical reasonable thinking will tell you. "Given my circumstances, given my environment, given what life has dealt me, I shouldn't be doing what I'm doing right now."

The first things I learned from my mother are that you must know within yourself that you can do it even without evidence and that you must make the commitment to do it. And the other very important thing she taught me is that you've got to be positive about life. You've got to feel and affirm constantly, that things can happen for you, positively. My mother used to say when times were very hard for us, "It's not going to be this way always. Things are going to get better. Real soon." "When Mama?" "I don't know when, but real soon." She used to say to my brother and me, "You're going to be something. You're going to be somebody."

I had been labeled "educable mentally retarded," which is a special education term rarely used anymore. The way I overcame this label was key for me because I came in contact with the man that changed my life in a very real and positive way. I was waiting for my friend who was in a school play being directed by Mr. Leroy Washington, a Speech and Drama teacher at our high school. I had been coming there many times to meet up with him, listening to all the lines of the various plays, waiting for my friend. This day, he didn't show up and Mr. Washington asked me to do something. I told him, "I can't do that, sir." He said, "Why not?" I told him that I was in another class, which was a special education class. He said, "It doesn't matter. Go to the board and follow my directions." I didn't want to embarrass myself and I said, "I can't do that, sir." He said, "Why not?" I said, "Because I'm educable mentally retarded."

He looked at me, came from around his desk, stared at me and said, "Don't ever say that again. Someone's opinion of you does not have to become your reality." While I was humiliated on one hand, I felt liberated on the other. I realized that most people live within the context of the ideas and the opinions that people have of us. I think that a lot of people have dropped out of life because someone told them something they couldn't do or they weren't good enough and they believed them. I realized that someone's opinion of me did not matter, that what people think about me is not really important. What is important is what I think about myself. It's so important to check out what kinds of thoughts, opinions and feelings you have about you. The limitations that you have and the negative things that you've internalized have been given to you by the world. The things that will empower you are things you have to give yourself. You've got to give yourself that love. You've got to turn that energy that you have into self-love, rather than self-destruction. You've got to tell yourself, "There is something special in me, some basic goodness. I have a right to manifest it. I have an obligation to manifest it everywhere I can, in my family life, the workplace, on the planet, and a responsibility to find some cause I can contribute to because I can make a difference on this earth."

I think that you can exist in a negative environment and that you have a choice not to allow that to exist in you. It amazes many people that I'm not a recovering drug addict or alcoholic since I've lived around it. Drugs, marijuana, alcohol, it never fazed me. I cannot ever remember being offered drugs by anyone that knows me. The only people who ever offered me any drugs or alcohol did not know me. We can't always control the hand that we're dealt in certain situations, but we can always control who we are. Many people punk out on themselves, they give up on who they are in deference to a strong personality in the crowd. People want to be loved, to be liked, to be popular, to be accepted. I believe that the lower your self-appreciation is, the greater your need to be accepted and loved by others. It's so important that we start early empowering ourselves and having people around us that can help us feel our own sense of specialness and uniqueness. I had a strong sense of purpose in my life. I knew that I was going to be somebody and that I was going to do something special with my life. The drugs and alcohol, the poverty and hopelessness that I saw was not for me. This was not my destiny. There were bigger and better things for me. How was I going to get there? I didn't know. It was my dream, constantly.

That's why it's so important for us to hold this vision of who we want to be and where we want to go. I used to dream about it, holding that vision in the future. As a young boy I listened to the radio a lot and I especially admired national news commentator Paul Harvey who broadcast across the country. I was also enthralled by the local disc jockeys, these very animated personalities on radio in Miami, Florida—Milton "Butterball" Smith, Nighthawk, Fred Hannah, the Nick with a Solid Kick, and Wildman Steve. These solid entertainers, musicians, and artists fascinated and captured the imagination of kids who listened to radio at that particular time and I wanted to become a disc jockey.

Mr. Washington, now my drama teacher, used to say that once you open your mouth, you tell the world who you are. He talked about the power of the spoken word and the importance of developing yourself and developing your vocabulary. Being labeled "educable mentally retarded" meant that kids teased us and called us dodos. I started to expand my vocabulary so that I would throw them off. I read the dictionary every day, memorized words and developed little rhymes. It helped my popularity and I had fun when asked my name saying, "Hey, they call me Mr. Vocabulary. Linguistically or rationally, I emphatically possess an ad infinitum etymology."

I started working to develop myself as a speaker, wanting to be like Mr. Washington, who was an eloquent speaker. After high school I was working for the Miami Sanitation Department, but still connected with Mr. Washington—who was helping me to develop my voice. I used to participate in various plays that he was producing. I decided to become a disc jockey, something I had always wanted to do. I always enjoyed talking to people. Finally, I decided to go and apply for a job at a local radio station. I saw the DJ Milton "Butterball" Smith, who everyone called Butterball, coming out. "How you doing Mr. Butterball?" I asked him.

He said, "Fine."

I said, "My name is Les Brown. I'd like to apply for a job as a disc jockey."

He looked at me, still in my work overalls and straw hat—I was working for the sanitation department and cutting the grass on Miami Beach. He said, "Do you have any experience?"

"No, sir. I don't," I answered.

"Do you have any journalism background?"

I said, "No, sir. I don't."

He said, "We don't have any job for you."

When I told Mr. Washington he said, "It's okay. Don't take it personally. Some people are so negative, they have to say no seven times before they say yes. So, go back to him again."

I went back again and said, "Hello, Mr. Butterball. How are you doing?"

He said, "Fine. What do you want now?"

I said, "I'd like to know whether or not you have any jobs available."

"Did I not just tell you yesterday, we didn't have any jobs?"

"Yes, sir," I replied, "but I thought maybe that somebody got sick or somebody got laid off."

"Nobody got sick or laid off. We don't have any jobs."

I left and I came back again like I'd seen him for the first time and I said, "Hello, Mr. Butterball. How are you doing?"

He said, "What do you want to know, young man? I'm busy."

"Do you have any jobs available?" I asked.

"Did I not just tell you yesterday and day before, we didn't have any jobs?"

"I thought maybe somebody died or got laid off or fired."

"No one died or got laid off. Leave me alone. I don't have time to mess with you."

"Yes, sir," I said and I left. Then I came back the next day like I was seeing him for the first time and I said, "Hello, Mr. Butterball. How are you? My name is Les Brown."

He said, "I know what your name is. Go get me some coffee, make yourself useful." And I did that. I went to get his coffee. Mr. Washington said, "If you want more out of life," he said, "you've got to be willing to pay your dues."

I became the errand boy for the station, I got their coffee and dinner. After a while, they began to trust me. I would bring the food into the control room and I would not leave until they would ask me to. I got to pick up entertainers that came to town, driving Donna Ross and the Supremes, the Four Tops, Sam Cooke, and The Temptations all over Miami Beach in the disc jockeys Cadillacs. I was paying my dues. Then one day, while I was at the radio station, one of the DJs was drinking while he was on the air. There I was at the radio station, hungry. I believe if you want more out of life, you've got to be hungry.

There I was at the station, watching through the control room window. I was ready. I was young and I was hungry. Pretty soon, the phone rang and the general manager said, "Les, Rock can't finish his program. Would you get one of the other disc jockeys to come in? Would you call them up?" I hung up the phone. I called my mom and my girlfriend and said, "You all come out on the front porch and turn up the radio. I'm about to come on the air." I waited for about 15 to 20 minutes then called back and said, "Mr. Klein, I can't find anybody." He said, "Young boy, do you know how to work the controls?" I said, "Yes sir." "Well you just go on in then," he told me.

I couldn't wait to sit down behind that turntable. I spoke into the microphone: "Look up! This is me— LBPPP—Les Brown, your Platter Playing Poppa. There were none before me and there will be none after me. Therefore, that makes me the one and only, young and single, love to mingle, certified, bona fide, and indubitably qualified, to bring you satisfaction, a whole lot of action. Look out babe, I'm your love, man." I was hungry. If you want more out of life, you have to be hungry. You've got to be willing to spend the time to burn the midnight oil, to rehearse and to practice, to make calls again and again and again.

When everybody else gets tired and ready to go home, you've got to be hungry enough that you refuse to give up, that you become a no-matter-what person, that you set some goals for yourself. You have an "I'm going to achieve these goals no matter what" attitude. I was determined to get into broadcasting. I got in there and I did it because I refused to be denied. I was hungry.

It was thrilling to have this breakthrough and get my start as a DJ in the radio world. I had reached an important goal I'd set for myself as a young child. As you reach milestones along your path to your dream, it's important to be aware of the unavoidable obstacles that are likely to emerge during your journey. When you're working on your goals and challenges in life, it's inevitable that you're going to have some setbacks. You're going to experience some disappointments. This will happen to most of us at some point. I suffered a major setback in my career. I can really identify with the millions of people who have lost their jobs, through closures, economic downturns, or being displaced through restructurings or downsizing. It is particularly difficult when you've been doing something all of your life and you feel that's all that you know how to do. There I was, at the top of my career and I lost my job. I was fired out of broadcasting and broadcasting was my life. It was everything to me.

I was a disc jockey in Ohio and I also became an on-air community commentator. I was editorializing about a lot of community issues and many of my opinions were controversial. I was reluctant to hold back from sharing my thoughts which led to the station terminating my employment. I had to make some crucial decisions about what I was going to do. It was a very depressing and challenging time. I worked very hard at staying busy. I did not want to stop doing things, to become overwhelmed by the problem I was facing. That's a slippery slope towards anger, negativity and bitterness. I did not want to start feeling sorry for myself or get down on myself. I started using my energy positively. Whenever my mother suffered any type of setback or disappointment she kept on going, she just kept on doing. So I just kept moving, trying to figure out what I was going to do next. A friend who worked at the station made an outlandish suggestion, "You always like to help people. You ought to run for political office."

"What do I know about political office?" I said.

He replied, "Most people don't know anything about political office when they run, and they learn when they get there." I thought he had to be kidding but he assured me it was true so I thought, "Why not?" Once again, I was willing to stretch, I was willing to grow. The day before the filing deadline I decided to run for State Representative in Columbus, Ohio. I told myself that I can do this.

We have the ability to do other things that we can never, ever begin to imagine we could do until we challenge ourselves. This was another stretch for me and I decided, "I can do it, why not?" I became a student. I started doing research in the political arena, just like I did when I prepared to go into broadcasting. I started going to the legislature, sitting up in the galleries and watching the legislative process. Listening to the men and women there, I decided, "If they can do it, I can do it." I ran for office. I worked every day. I spent eight to ten hours a day going door to door. When I was in broadcasting I had a saying, "Stand up for what you believe in because you can fall for anything." As I ran for office I said, "Tell everybody you know that Les Brown is still standing."

I beat the incumbent and served in the Ohio State Legislature from the 29th House District, and I eventually became the Chairman of the Human Resource Committee during my third term. During my first term I introduced and passed more legislation than any other representative up to that time in the history of the Ohio legislature.

What was different for me? I decided that there was life after broadcasting, that I could do something else. I ventured into another arena and I challenged myself to learn something else. I believe that wherever you are right now, you have the talents and abilities to go into another arena. As you challenge yourself to discover that higher self within you, you will find things you didn't even know you had in you. When you put yourself in a position where you have to stretch, when you go outside of your comfort zone, you will call forth powers and talents that have been lying dormant within you. Releasing these abilities gives a feeling of accomplishment, a sense of purpose and personal power that words cannot describe. There's more in you than you are now expressing. Jim Rohn says something that stops me in my tracks every time I hear it, "Can you imagine getting to the end of your life and looking back to discover that you only used 10% of what was given you?"

I've decided that I want life to use me up. I hope that is your decision as well, to allow life to use you up. We don't want our tombstone to read, "Dead but not used up yet." My hope for you is that you don't take anything with you but leave everything here that you've brought to the planet, to enrich us all.

twelve

PUT IT ALL TOGETHER

As we look around us and observe life, we begin to know that this is a great time to be alive. As we begin to seize the moment where we are and move into the future, it's a good time to start saying yes to ourselves. As you begin to develop a larger vision of yourself, you start to say "yes" to your life. I like the story of Fred Luster, an average man who took a dream and used it to make a difference, not only for himself but for others. Fred Luster was laid off from his job a steel worker. He took this setback and challenged himself to try something else. He learned to become a barber and eventually was inspired to develop a line of hair care products catering to his customers' needs. This man who was not college educated or trained in business built his store-front operation into a multi-million-dollar worldwide enterprise, Luster Products, that is still standing today.

Look at yourself right now and know that you can change your personal history, regardless of what you have experienced, regardless of what your circumstances are or have been. You have the capacity to reinvent yourself right now. You created what you are right now and you have the capacity to rewrite your script because you are the star of your life. You are the screenwriter, the producer. You are directing this life and you determine if your life is going to be a flop or smash hit. What is it? Is your life giving you what you want? If it's not, guess who can change that? You can.

You can change the direction of your life. It is so important to have powerful goals. Many people don't know what they want and are just drifting aimlessly through life. They don't know where they're going. If you're aiming at nothing you usually end up hitting nothing right on the head. Start thinking and asking, what do I want in my personal life, in my career, in my business life, what do I want physically? What kind of body do I want? Do I like what I have right now? What are my strengths? What are my weaknesses? What would make me happy? People say, "I just want to be happy." How does that show up for you? "I want a whole lot of money." What's a whole lot of money to you? "I want a job where I'd be satisfied." What is that? "I want to go into business for myself." What kind of business? You can't be vague about these goals, you want to be exact, you want to be clear and exact on what it is that you want, and then write them down.

Put together a plan of action and start working on those plans. If that doesn't work, you change the strategy and start working on that new plan. But first you must become clear on where you're going. There's an old saying, "If you don't know where you're going, you're going to end up someplace else." What's very important is a commitment to be happy. High school principal, Charles L. Williams said, "Love and happiness are perfumes that you can sprinkle on others without getting a few drops on yourself." I'm reminded of Mildred Singleton whose husband died right before she had to take the test to become a doctor. I asked her, "What did you do? How did you clear your mind? How did you handle it?" She said that in the midst of that tragedy she kept focused on the dream that she had as one of eight children. Her father gave her $100 and said, "Go to school. If you make all As, somebody will give you a scholarship." She believed him and did just that. She got good grades and a scholarship. Her dream was to become an ophthalmologist. When she was on a school field trip to a hospital she saw some doctors working on a patient's eyes and at that moment saw her destiny. So when she was experiencing her great heart-break with the loss of her husband, she said, "At that lowest point, all I did was could do was think about what was could give me the greatest happiness. Being a doctor, helping people to have better vision brings me the greatest joy. Just the thought of it brings a smile to my face." She focused, thought about her dream, and passed the exam.

If you want to manifest your greatness and begin to move into the true person that you have it within you to be, you've got to select the right people. It takes a lot of energy to reach your goals, to stay focused, to handle the challenges of life. When the storms of life come, when the messenger of misery visits you, you want to have a support team to buffer you. You want to have people around you when life knocks you down and that's going to happen. When life catches you on the blind side you want people around you that will cheer you on, "Come on, Joe, you can do it. Come on, Lillian, get up. You've got what it takes." When life knocks you down again, you want to have people around you that will give you the determination to land on your back, because if you can look up, you can get up, so be very selective. Look often at the people in your life and evaluate them, review what kind of impact they're having on you. Are you growing? Decide that you want to associate with the people that can bring out the best in you, people who will challenge you to do more, to achieve more, to stretch yourself. When I aspired to become a speaker, I joined the National Speakers Association because I wanted to be around the best in my profession, the people who decided to develop mastery and recognition in this field. What is it that you want to do? Seek out the people that are doing it the way you want to do it and learn from them.

Whatever goal that you have, decide that you're not going to sit on your dream, decide to do whatever it takes in order to make it. What means that much to you? What means so much to you that whatever it takes, you're willing to face the test; you're willing to take the chance? Make the commitment. What is it? Find something because that something will give you your very life. It will enable you to become a powerful person, to transcend yourself. Honoring yourself and the best in yourself makes us the most powerful of all.

Each of us has some basic goodness, which is the foundation upon which we can begin to produce greatness on the planet. Right now there is greatness within you just waiting for you to bring it into expression, regardless of what you produced in the past, "But Les, you don't know me, you don't know my shortcomings. You don't know what I've done, the mistakes I've made." None of that really matters. The only thing that matters is what you are going to do with the rest of your life.

As you challenge yourself, as you work on your goals, as you make a commitment to seek out a level of happiness you are doing that which you're supposed to do. As you work consciously, deliberately, patiently and faithfully to reinvent yourself realize that you have the power to live your dreams, to continue to say "yes" to life even when things are telling you "no." Realize that you are a powerful person and though there will be times when you get knocked down, you won't be knocked out. You will honor yourself and continue to move forward.

We live in a great country that enables us to make a contribution and to make a difference. We are here and experience a great deal of benefit because at some point in time, somebody made a supreme sacrifice. All of us have a responsibility and obligation to give something back. Think about how you can be an asset, who is it that you could help? What good can you contribute? You have something to give, find a cause you can take a stand on.

How do you get unstuck, Les? I've been doing the best I could. I've been trying to give but I need myself. I've been going through challenges. I'm having all kinds of problems in my life right now. There are times I can't even pay my bills. There are times I'm filled with fear. There are times seemed like the harder I work, the deeper the hole gets that I'm trying to get out of. What do you do when you don't know what to do?

The things you should do, you don't do and the things you shouldn't do, you do. Sometimes it just seems like my life is in shamble, it's a disaster. Nothing's working. How do you get out of that rut that people call the open grave. First, look at what brought you here; look at what you've been doing that produced the results you have in your life now. Remember, in life you don't get what you want, you get what you are. Take responsibility for what you are. Earl Nightingale said, "We are all self-made, but only the successful will admit it." All of us are responsible for the results in our lives, but only the successful people admit that. People who are falling short of their dreams, who look at their lives in disaster hate to own up to the fact that they created it. Ego and pride won't permit us to do that. I'll never forget when I was going through a major challenge in my life and I was down and out and I had a friend who talked to me honestly. He said, "Les, guess who created this mess for you? I know you're angry and I know you're upset. Point your finger at any number of things or people but ultimately, you have three fingers pointing back at you. You created this and it doesn't have to be this way for you. But let me tell you something, things are not going to get better for you until you get better. No one else can make that happen."

We all have shortcomings, we're all going to make mistakes, we're going to experience some disappointments and some failures. Why? It goes with the territory of being a human being. Does that mean we're supposed to stop? Of course, not. There are times you're going to want to give up, times you'll feel deserted, people will lie and won't keep their commitments. You're going to run out of resources. All of that is a part of it, and that's how you grow. That's how you learn from life. Whatever you're experiencing right now, it has not come to stay. It has come to pass. You'll be a bigger and better person, because of your "take it on, don't run from it" attitude. Embrace it, step into it. Charles Udall said that, "In life, you'll always be faced with a series of God-ordained opportunities brilliantly disguised as problems and challenges." This God-ordained opportunity is challenging you to bring out the very best in you. Begin to work consciously to get unstuck. Find a cause that brings meaning to your life, work to develop the powerful person you have within you and decide to do whatever is required. When you make up your mind to do whatever is required that can mean changing relationships, letting go of some people and situations in your life.

Life is very challenging. It's not easy living your dream. It's not easy saying "yes" to life. It's not easy reinventing yourself. It's not easy sticking to and focusing on your goal. It's not easy being happy in the midst of a great deal of negativity. It's not easy to remove people from your life that are no longer good for you. It's not easy doing all the things that are required. When you experience defeat and failure, it's not easy to pull yourself back up and start all over again. It's not easy to be the powerful person that you have within you to be when you've been told so many times about your limitations not your potential. It's not easy to see that you can make a difference, to get unstuck and move on into your true greatness, when all your life you've been living in an illusion that you're mediocre. It takes a great deal of courage to face yourself and say, "No, my life is not what I want it to be and I can change." That's not easy and yet you have all you need right within you and you can do it.

Be in the moment where you are right now with what you have. Make the commitment to be happy now, not one day in the future, but right now. Find those goals that mean something to you. Write them out, read them every day, and develop a plan of action. Make up your mind that you have the power within you to reinvent you, as you say "yes" to your dreams. That is what brings you to a new level of courage to begin to really truly enjoy life.

I think about you and the courage that is going to be required for you to begin to bring it all together. I know you can do it. When the end comes for you, let it find you conquering a new mountain, reaching for the stars and leaving the best you have behind for all of us. This is Mrs. Mamie Brown's baby boy, Leslie Calvin Brown saying it's been a plum pleasing pleasure as well as a privilege to say "yes" to your dreams.

Printed in the USA
CPSIA information can be obtained
at www.ICGtesting.com
JSHW012032140824
68134JS00033B/3018